DO WHAT YOU LOVE

And Other Lies About
Success and Happiness

MIYA TOKUMITSU

Regan Arts.
NEW YORK

Regan Arts.

65 Bleecker Street
New York, NY 10012

First Regan Arts hardcover edition, August 2015.

Library of Congress Control Number: 2014955554

ISBN 978-1-941393-47-5

Interior design by Nancy Singer
Jacket design by Richard Ljoenes

Printed in the United States of America

10 9 8 7 6 5 4 3 2 1

CONTENTS

INTRODUCTION

A person who works in an art by which he can attain both profit and virtue together must count himself lucky.

—Cornelis de Bie, *The Golden Cabinet of the Noble and Liberal Art of Painting*, 1662[1]

Rome, 1509. Michelangelo was not enjoying himself. Instead, he was painting the ceiling of the Sistine Chapel, twisting and craning his body into awkward positions while irritating drops of paint fell on his face. In a poem addressed to his friend Giovanni da Pistoia, he complains, "I've grown a goiter from this trap I'm in," and "In front I feel my skin stretched lengthwise, but in back it crimps and folds. This is my state: arched and indented like a Syrian bow." Troubling, too, was his mental state: he wrote of "strange thoughts" that ran through his mind, which were "not to be trusted." Throwing his proverbial hands up in the air, Michelangelo concludes his missive, "I am not in the right place—I am not a painter."[2]

Michelangelo's words are at once familiar and surprising.

Everybody has bad days at work, days when our work truly does feel like a trap with no discernible escape, and it's amusing to hear an august figure voice, through the space of five-hundred years, the same quotidian complaints people grumble about today. There's humor in that universal grumpiness about work, as well as the opportunity for human connection through camaraderie and commiseration. But perhaps what's so shocking for us to hear is that even for this great artist, the ceiling of the Sistine Chapel, one of the most beloved artworks in the Western canon—was a product of labor[3]: both the anxious, self-doubting mental labor of planning and organizing such a complex work, and the aching, sweaty labor of applying pigment under papal directive.

The mythologies of artistic labor, as fueled by passion, genius, mental illness, faith, drug abuse, longing, mystical visions, and, of course, love, is vast. But, ultimately, all of these romanticized motivations are masks, hiding the simple fact that work is work, even if it produces something cherished or beautiful. In fact, most "sublime" and "heavenly" products of human artifice, from temples to concertos, also involve a painful panoply of goiters, spasms, eyestrain, and blisters. And then there are the mental anguishes of exasperation and tedium. While such works may be inflected by individual genius, they are also documents of historical power structures with their own specific expectations and limitations. As art historian Michael Baxandall writes in the opening of his classic book, *Painting and Experience in Fifteenth-Century Italy*, "A fifteenth-century painting is the deposit of a social relationship."[4] Whatever Michelangelo's motivations for painting the Sistine Chapel's ceiling—wages, renown, it's hard to say no to a pope—love for the work of ceiling painting was not among them.

Our myths about what motivates us to work extend far beyond the visual arts. Today, one of the most powerfully appealing narratives about work is the one about the worker who performs work that he or she loves. These ideal workers become successful and wealthy precisely because they love their work, which they committed to through a rational and impediment-free decision-making process that led them to the most perfect and enjoyable way to spend the hours between 9 and 6. In this story, wealth, pleasure, and work are intertwined and inseparable. It's a seductive trinity—one that beckons to each new generation—and indeed it has inspired great sacrifices by those striving to live up to it.

Central to the myth of work-as-love is the notion that virtue (moral righteousness of character) and capital (money) are two sides of the same coin. Where there is wealth, there is the hard work, the industriousness, and the individualistic dash of ingenuity that makes it possible. Such logic is the very bedrock of the American Dream and similar ideas about striving social mobility around the globe. Apply oneself according to these principles, hold fast to them amid the fickle gales of the free market, and, as Willy Loman tells his boys in *Death of a Salesman*, "The greatest things can happen!" If only.

The virtues of pursuing capital are fluid, and they have changed over time. The seemingly fixed qualities that we value—hard work and industriousness—once required the deferral of pleasure, the sacrifice of immediate gratification for future reward, perhaps awaiting us in the afterlife. Well into the twentieth century, work was virtuous precisely because it was not fun, because it was in the service of a project grander and more eternal than fleeting individual pleasure. This particular imagining of virtuous work is embedded in America's foundational mythology. Although he owned a plantation cultivated by slave labor, Thomas Jefferson sketched a pastoral, if highly paternalistic, vision of subsistence farm labor in *Notes on the State of Virginia* (1785): "Those who labor in the earth are the chosen people of God, if ever he had a chosen people whose breasts he has made his particular deposit for substantial and genuine virtue." Jefferson's imaginary cultivators are free from moral corruption because they work in a precapitalist mode; these independent farmers do not depend on "the casualties and caprice of customers"[5] for their well-being and are thus sheltered from the free market's hucksterism and dirty games. Nowhere does Jefferson claim that farming is fun (if it were, plantation owners wouldn't have to enslave others to do it); instead, because subsistence farming is totally consuming labor—the farmer must constantly tend to "his own soil and industry"—he becomes virtuous through his disengagement from worldly machinations.

Today, ideal work *is* the combined pursuit of pleasure and capital. Fantastically popular embodiments of wealth and success, like Oprah Winfrey, openly and proudly proclaim their success to be the product of self-love. Winfrey exhorts her fans to "live your best life." Whole Foods CEO John Mackey explicitly links love and corporate success, asserting that "love creates creative competitive advantage in a healthy marketplace."[6] On the surface, today's promises of work seem so much more thrilling than those of previous generations. Why settle for a thirty-year fixed-rate mortgage and a perfectly functional eight-year-old car when you can get rich becoming your "best" self and have a blast along the way?

And yet despite the love talk, workers today are doing more for less. Real household income in the United States has stagnated or fallen for the overwhelming majority of Americans, even as they put in more hours on the job, or jobs, as is increasingly the case. Benefits are eroding rapidly, and workers are losing control over the conditions of their labor regarding everything from scheduling to safety regulations. Meanwhile, wealth continues to concentrate in the hands of a tiny few not because of wages earned, but, as Thomas Piketty recently showed, because capital grows in value far more quickly than does wage income. Owning, not working, is what generates the most significant wealth. Yet, while winner-take-all capitalism grows ever more ruthless, rhetorics of love, passion, and bliss regarding waged labor proliferate. Are we all just delusional?

Perhaps, but it's hard to step outside of the work-as-love hall of mirrors we've constructed for ourselves. Seductive slogans about work as self-actualization and images of blissful labor are ubiquitous. "Where passion leads, success follows" announces a placard advertising an MBA program on a commuter train. *Cosmopolitan* magazine runs a regular feature "Get That Life" profiling young women with quirky, fun careers: bridal boutique owner, urban farmer/artist. The very title "Get That Life," explicitly fetishizes the cool job, holding it up as an object of desire while simultaneously making it beguilingly accessible. The cool job is there, waiting for you. All you, the reader, have to do is "get" it—even though many of the profiled women have prestigious (expensive) degrees, professional connections, and ample specialized experience. Projections of work-as-love have also seeped into the realm of low-wage service work: a maid-service company advertising on Craigslist is currently looking for "a passionate individual" to clean houses. A couple of generations ago a similar ad might have used the word *responsible*.

Considering the vast disjunction between popular fantasies about work and the actual returns work provides most workers today, it's time to put these "do what you love" (DWYL) tropes under the microscope. I have argued elsewhere[7] that DWYL is an essentially narcissistic schema, facilitating willful ignorance of working conditions of others by encouraging continuous self-gratification. I have also argued that DWYL exposes its adherents to exploitation, justifying unpaid or underpaid work by throwing workers' motivations back at them; when *passion* becomes the socially accepted motivation for working, talk of wages or reasonable scheduling becomes crass. This book examines the many expectations about what work can provide under the DWYL creed, and the sacrifices that workers make in order to meet those expectations.

In the first chapter, I discuss how work defines our visibility in the public sphere. A job title is typically how we announce ourselves to the public; it determines who will or won't acknowledge a person at a party or on social media, whether or not a person is "interesting." I examine the issue of worker invisibility and visibility through depictions of workers consumed as popular entertainment, specifically in two television series, *The Good Wife* and *Enlightened*, in which the protagonists experience drastic changes in their status as workers and in their public profiles. The second chapter focuses on fantasies of worker autonomy and the current rise of deeply intrusive management and surveillance techniques. While workers strive for jobs that grant them large degrees of self-determination, much of today's professional work, from teaching to law, is becoming drastically de-skilled while pressures to outwardly declare satisfaction with this work intensifies. How can we understand this tension? Chapter 3 examines hope as a motivation for uncompensated or undercompensated work across the employment landscape. Secure, well-compensated jobs are dangled just beyond the reach of unpaid interns, temp workers, and adjunct faculty in higher education. This chapter unspools the rhetoric of love and hope in order to reveal its true, disciplinary function: to extract cheap work from a labor force that embraces its own exploitation. The final chapter critiques DWYL's justifications for our contemporary culture of overwork, the will to work extreme schedules that encroach upon our emotional and biological needs for relationships, care, and sleep. It exposes the false logics of overwork, namely that it is unproductive and therefore undervalues the very work it proclaims to serve and debunks classist myths about who is and isn't actually working the most extreme "heroic" schedules.

Among the promises of "lovable" work are public visibility, social mobility, and worker autonomy. To have even a grasp at them, today's workers need to sacrifice more than ever: they need to acquire costly credentials (usually in the form of degrees or certificates), to submit to intrusive surveillance, to put in undercompensated work and "pay their dues," proving their love for a specific profession, and of course to work longer hours. Do all of the above and just maybe a worker can join the ranks of the stably employed and comfortably compensated, perhaps even while enjoying the work.

THE MORALITY OF LOVABLE WORK

How did love, pleasure, fun, and constant attention to the self's desires become the picture of ideal work? How did they overtake self-sacrifice as virtues? Even more fundamentally, how did work become seen as worthy in itself, as one of the widely accepted parts of human existence?

At the crux of these questions is the so-called work ethic, the idea that morality is manifest in a person's approach toward work, and how society has understood and internalized the work ethic at different points in time. In 1905, the German sociologist Max Weber made the still-resonant argument in *The Protestant Ethic and the Spirit of Capitalism* that the values of austere Protestantism—industrious pursuit of wealth, deferral of pleasure, subjugation of individual desire, acceptance of obligation—defined a capitalist "spirit" in which work and the acquisition of wealth were noble ends in and of themselves. Weber astutely described the relationship between virtue and capital in America, particularly, via his close reading of Benjamin Franklin's *Necessary Hints to Those That Would Be Rich* (1736) and *Advice to a Young Tradesman* (1748). In these texts,

Franklin urges readers to constantly refine their behavior and habits, and, especially, the *appearance* of their behavior and habits, in ways amenable to the accrual of capital and credit. Weber writes, "Now, all Franklin's moral attitudes are colored with utilitarianism. Honesty is useful, because it assures credit; so are punctuality, industry, frugality, and that is the reason they are virtues."[8]

These virtues shape and are shaped by capitalist enterprise. Weber notes that, although impulses like greed and covetousness transcend time and geography, "a state of mind as that expressed [by Franklin], and which called forth the applause of a whole people, would both in ancient times and the Middle Ages have been proscribed as the lowest sort of avarice and as an attitude entirely lacking in self-respect."[9] The capitalist spirit puts man in service of his work, whereas previously this relationship was the reverse.

Franklin's gospel of self-improvement via enterprise took root in the American psyche and blossomed. The foundations of this value system—that work is inherently moral, and earnings a reflection of character—remain firm to this day. Not that it went unchallenged. In the intervening generations, significant movements of resistance to this value system have arisen: powerful labor organizations that fought for shorter working hours and derided job creation for its own sake as "make work,"[10] active socialist and communist parties in the nineteenth and twentieth centuries, a civil rights movement that fought racialized economic injustice, to name a few. Today, however, belief in morally self-serving work has reasserted itself with vigor. The difference between today's version and Franklin's, however, lies in what constitutes virtuous striving. Franklin's punctuality, frugality, and industry all require the diminishment of the self to some extent, and the repression of immediate desires. Passion for the tasks of work was irrelevant. In fact, the less enjoyable the work, the better. In *Cubed: A Secret History of the Office*, Nikil Saval discusses a best-selling pamphlet of the 1880s "Blessed Be Drudgery," written by Christian evangelist William Gannett. Drudgery may not be pleasant, Gannett argued, but it is what produces all of life's comforts and refinements. For this reason workers should be glad of it.[11] Today, tedious work is a fate to be avoided if at all possible. "Blessed Be Drudgery" has been knocked off the shelf long ago by tracts like Marsha Sinetar's 1987 book, *Do What You Love and the Money Will Follow*.

Happiness, love, passion, and self-fulfillment are today's work virtues. "The only way to do great work is to love what you do," assured former Apple CEO Steve Jobs, "great work" striking the ear as only the slightest shade removed from Christian "good works." What an appealing message! Work that is fun, that the worker loves, that indulges the worker's individual predilections, not only generates wealth, but is also, by mere dint of being enjoyable, good. In fact, lovable work is the only work that can be great. No delay of gratification, sacrifice, or consideration of the needs of others is necessary. Jobs was hardly alone in delivering this message. When it comes to work, "follow your bliss," advises CNN anchor Anderson Cooper, repeating the advice that his mother gave him when he was a young Yale graduate pondering his future. Never mind if that bliss might require a trust fund to truly follow it, or if it's at odds with the needs of one's community, or if it's outright harmful to others. (What if your bliss is international weapons smuggling?) How did such single-minded dedication to individual pleasure become the path to moral work, overtaking frugality and modesty?

The children of the post-WWII years completely remade Franklin's gospel. In 1976, Tom Wolfe synthesized the changes he observed unfolding in American subjectivity in a famous essay for *New York* magazine, "The 'Me' Decade and the Third Great Awakening." Wolfe wrote, "The old alchemical dream was turning base metals into gold. The new alchemical dream is: changing one's personality—remaking, remodeling, elevating, and polishing one's very *self* . . . and observing, studying, doting on it. (Me!)."[12]

America's postwar government had spread unprecedented amounts of money to nearly "every class level of the population" except the chronically poor. The "common man" (whom we understand to be white) was now in possession of "the things he needed to realize his potential as a human being: surplus (discretionary) income, political freedom, free time (leisure), and freedom from grinding drudgery."[13] However, rather than apply these resources toward making a revolutionary, more egalitarian society for all, workers administered them toward the self-indulgences previously denied them, namely the pastime of dwelling on themselves. Refinement of taste and behavior had once been limited to the aristocracy and the wealthy bourgeoisie; by the second half of the twentieth century, this was no longer the case. More equitable leisure time and disposable income had allowed attending to one's peculiarities to go middlebrow.[14]

Wolfe notes that many of the *"me* movements" of the 1970s, practiced through the various prisms of psychoanalysis, psychedelic experience, Eastern religion, Western religion, Scientology, or some combination of the above, focused practitioners on locating some kind of real, authentic *me* and hence took on a spiritual, righteous dimension. Which is precisely where they join up with the Protestant spirit of capitalism. If work and the pursuit of capital are righteous, and unceasing self-discovery is righteous, then surely it is ideal to pursue capital *while* attending to oneself. Thus DWYL became in the popular imagination not a luxury or a privilege, but a duty and an expectation. It became *good.*

This intensified focus on *me* has had cultural consequences beyond redefining the Protestant work ethic as DWYL. It underlies everything from a popular strain of libertarianism that defines freedom in terms of individual self-determination to the self-help culture that dominates best-seller lists. It falsely ascribes "choice" as the ultimate cause of every single condition of individuals' lives. If people are successful because they "choose" lucrative work that they love, then people must also "choose" to be poor and exploited. Hence President Ronald Reagan's relentless condemnation of the poor, insisting that they were all welfare cheats purposefully leeching off of the taxpaying public. Reagan's invective proved wildly popular, a rousing dose of affirmation to his base of white, middle-class and wealthy voters (as well as those who aspired to join their ranks), thirsty for validation after decades of criticism coming from the civil rights and antiwar movements.

The Protestant work ethic never made much room for empathy, but the utter blitheness with which the insistently positive DWYL ethos and "me" culture leave it out is chilling. Complaining about exploitation and demanding better treatment aren't sinful doubts of God's will, they're just a bummer. After all, instead of grumbling, workers can simply, individually choose a different line of work, better pay, a more comfortable and "fulfilling" life.

So what's stopping everyone from going out and having

fun and making money and being good people? Well, it turns out that there are a few things one has to do first.

THE DOWN PAYMENT: DEBT AND CREDENTIALS

Shortly after he graduated from his expensive liberal arts program, writer Aaron Braun had a job . . . "at the Columbia University Barnes & Noble, where I unpacked Homer and Locke for incoming freshmen."[15] Although most college freshmen have no idea what the picture of their working lives will look like, it's probably safe to venture that box cutters and chain stores don't figure very prominently in them.

College is supposed to be the corridor to lovable work, typically performed by so-called knowledge workers. These workers earn lots of money—luxury sedan and kitchen remodeling money—not by swinging pickaxes or driving forklifts, but by using their minds. It is still largely true that the only way to join these fortunate ranks is to attend a liberal arts college or university. But more so than the mastery of any academic discipline (much to the dismay of many professors), it is the beacons of professionalism and upper-middle-class comfort that draw people to the liberal arts degree and motivate them to complete it. These promises are so alluring that people willingly pay actual fortunes to reach for them; today, more than fifty colleges and universities in the United States charge more than $60,000 for one year of tuition and fees.[16] People pay these prices not only because "the greatest things can happen!" upon graduation, but also because the costs of *not* obtaining at least some kind of secondary degree are so very dear.

Despite the heartburn-inducing cost of college tuition, degree holders will outearn nondegree holders over a lifetime of work. In 2013, workers with a four-year college degree earned 98 percent more per hour than those without, a pay gap that has widened over the years, even as tuition costs rise.[17] Furthermore, when the cost of college, even as high as it is, is subtracted from the difference in lifetime earnings between degree holders and nondegree holders, the number comes to $500,000. That is, in foregoing college, the penalty against lifetime earnings is half a million dollars.[18] So college is technically "worth it," but Robert Reich, the former secretary of labor under President Bill Clinton, points out that there is a big catch: yes, the wage gap between degree holders and nondegree holders is large and growing, but only because the latter's wages have dropped so sharply. Many college graduates hold jobs that don't actually require degrees, pushing nondegree holders into even lower-paid work, if they can find any at all. This trend has the effect of driving down wages overall.[19] Also, while the college degree is a prerequisite for joining the middle class, the middle class is hardly robust; its share of society's wealth continues to contract, while the share going to the very top increases.[20] "Given all this," Reich writes, "a college degree is worth the cost because it at least enables a young person to tread water."[21]

With decently paying manufacturing and service jobs a distant memory—exported, automated, or simply eliminated—forgoing a college degree dooms workers to a lifetime of extremely low-wage, largely contingent work and an overall existence defined by precariousness. In the United States, a particularly weak social safety net means that low-wage earners struggle inordinately for the most basic of needs, including food, shelter, and health care. (These trends are not limited to the United States; around the globe, governments are raising or deregulating university fees while simultaneously cutting social services.)

But do average American families have the ability to write checks for $60,000 or $30,000 or even $10,000 per child per year for four years? They do not. Largely for this reason, the undergraduate classes at top private, and, increasingly, at top state schools, hail primarily from the very not-average families with household incomes well into the six figures. Over half of Harvard University's class of 2017 reported their family's income to be between $125,000 and $250,000 per year; 14 percent of the class comes from families netting more than $500,000 per year. According to the US Census, the median American household income hovers around $50,000.[22] Admirably, Harvard and a handful of the wealthiest private schools provide generous grant-only financial aid. But what if your application dossier lacks the tutor-buffed test scores and squash court prowess to catch an Ivy League admissions officer's eye? Not to worry; there are thousands of higher-education institutions across the country, many of them more expensive than Harvard, and a menu of public and private loans to cover the cost of tuition. The history of federally backed loans for secondary-degree tuition is long and speckled early on with sanguine developments (healthily funded state schools, the GI Bill). I'll skip to the ending, though: today, student debt amounts to more than $1 trillion, eclipsing nearly all other forms of private debt in America, including credit card debt. Student debt, unlike other personal debt, cannot be discharged in bankruptcy. Default on private or federal student loans exposes debtors to invasive measures such as wage garnishment, interception of tax refunds and lottery winnings, and, most troublingly, the withholding of future Social Security payments.[23]

What does it mean to price the credentials needed for middle-class work in the tens of thousands of dollars? It means that the vast majority of professional workers will labor under heavy debt loads. They will be less free to innovate or challenge the status quo at work, regarding both the work output and the working conditions. "Disruption" is only for those with soft landings and few consequences. They will necessarily be more submissive and accepting of what work they can get, under whatever conditions are imposed on them. Make the cost of the credentials, and hence the debt, massive and inescapable, and a large portion of the workforce will labor under these conditions for decades, if not their entire working lives. The transformation of much of the middle class into a class of debtors is, as Chris Maisano writes, an insidious form of social control with a deceitfully cheery exterior:

> The genius of this form of social control is that it elicits the active participation of the population in the construction of its own discipline. By bringing ever-widening circles of the population into the orbit of finance capital, it imbues the process of financialization with a spirit that accords with democratic norms of mass participation and equal opportunity. After all, what could be more American than the proposition that everyone have access to a college education and, presumably, a chance to go as far as your talents can take you?[24]

Herein lies the initial treachery of DWYL, the falsely democratic exhortation of the "do," which seems to apply equally to everyone. Maybe anyone can do what he or she loves, but only the wealthy can avoid going into debt to pay for it.

These measures would be problematic and unjust even in

flush times. What makes them disastrous is that the very things that these earnest student debtors are paying to achieve—the professional job with the fat salary with which to pay their debts—have evaporated. Over the past decade wages for workers between ages 25 and 34 with bachelor's degrees have actually fallen 15 percent while student debt loads have grown by 24 percent.[25] That is, if new graduates can get a wage at all. Unpaid internships have infiltrated the professional landscape, depressing wages and providing additional barriers to careers in fields like the media, the arts, and government policy (though by no means limited to them). The entry-level *job*, in which rookies actually get paid to make photocopies and take minutes at meetings while learning the ropes of a profession, is on its way to becoming an antiquity. Other professional careers—in law, academia, medicine, journalism—often require additional degrees, meaning more debt.

Those lucky enough to find professional jobs often discover nonetheless that the conditions of this work hardly align with the dulcet promises of commencement speeches still ringing in their ears. Audiences hear that work can be—ought to be—the manifestation of passion, the fulfillment of dreams, the enactment of love, the improvement of self. For some, perhaps it will be, though even these fortunates will have to endure the occasional obnoxious client or the tedium of bookkeeping. However, many find that professional work hardly requires the use of expensively acquired analytical skills. Although the pay is good, young analysts in Wall Street's salt mines quickly learn that the main qualifications for their jobs are a facility with Microsoft Excel and a willingness to work three consecutive days without sleeping.[26] Freshly Ivy League–minted lawyers endure the scourge of "doc review"—scanning boxes of documents for flagged names and terms for sixteen-hour days at the country's fanciest law firms. These are the good professional jobs—if the young worker bees can just avoid burnout, disillusionment, or stalling out because of health issues, parenting or caretaking duties, or any of life's other curveballs, then wealth, public respect, and designer kitchens may indeed await.

Perhaps the problem is not work itself but bosses and corporations, and the remedy is the Instagram-filtered dream of entrepreneurship and self-employment. The images of this kind of work are beautiful and precious: a graphic designer working for herself in a hip urban studio, in Brooklyn . . . no, Berlin; a bakery owner selecting freshly milled flours in the golden morning light. However, the realities of this kind of work, too, are grim for those lacking in start-up cash or high-earning partners who can float them during the long slog to possible profitability. According to the New York Freelancers Union, in 2010 29 percent of its members in the city netted $25,000 or less in one of the world's most expensive cities, working in the so-called gig economy.[27] Without benefits. And many gigs themselves are not without credential requirements: to hold classes in one of New York City's biggest yoga studios, instructors need to complete a full-time, $12,000 training course, which they must pay for themselves.[28] Freelance editors and designers often need to disclose their degrees in order to obtain work. As for creative workers with ambitions of acclaim and autonomy, the rise of the MFA credentialized the performing, literary, and visual arts decades ago. Sure, the occasional "outsider artist" breaks through, but the pipeline to agents, galleries, fellowships, and other institutional support typically opens up with the tuition-financed credential.

Work is beginning to lose its shine. Increasing ranks of workers are finding their jobs, the credentials for which they have indebted themselves so deeply, to be de-skilled, dead-end, oppressively managed, low-paying, and never-ending. And yet for each of these conditions, there is some strand of DWYL to justify it. Bitter about getting home after 9 p.m. each day? You shouldn't want to stop work that you love. Frustrated that you can only find work on a contract basis after getting two or three degrees? Well, you should be doing it for love, not money. Each of the following chapters examines the expectations established and sacrifices demanded by the DWYL ethos, the conceit that waged work serves the self and not the marketplace. As long as our well-being depends on income, and income, for most, depends on work, love will always be secondary as a motivation for doing it. Encouraging workers to pretend otherwise is disingenuous and exploitative.

It is my sincere hope that all workers can find some source of pride and accomplishment in their work, whatever it is. But that can only happen when we acknowledge the contributions each worker makes instead of ignoring work that doesn't seem bliss-inducing, and make all work "lovable"—with sustainable wages, safe conditions, and humane schedules that include time for leisure and rest. A fortunate few may find the actual tasks of their work to be a source of love, but it is also everyone's right to find love elsewhere.

1

VISIBLE WORK and the PUBLIC PROFILE

Since our feeling for reality depends utterly upon appearance and therefore upon the existence of a public realm into which things can appear out of the darkness of sheltered existence, even the twilight which illuminates our private and intimate lives is ultimately derived from the much harsher light of the public realm.

—Hannah Arendt, *The Human Condition* (1958)

"You've got to find what you love," Steve Jobs insisted in his commencement speech to Stanford University's class of 2005. Jobs stood before his audience as an example of the fabulous success and adulation made possible by his own advice—his outsize iconic visibility. By doing what you love, not only can you be wealthy and by extension powerful, but also potentially adored by millions. The underlying message of "do what you love" is that each individual's specialness will guide him or her to work that he or she enjoys and that also happens to support, at the very least, an upper-middle-class existence. Central to this enjoyment is that the work allows a worker's specialness to be constantly showcased, and thus recognized, honored, monetized. Such work not only furnishes workers with salaries but also with socially prestigious public profiles, monikers of pride that guarantee that someone will listen when these workers speak. It offers ready-made, class-inflected identities: lawyer, editor, designer, financial analyst, engineer. It allows the worker to be visible in public.

Omitted from Jobs's speech were the thousands of Apple's manufacturing and support workers, many hidden from his Stanford audience on the other side of the planet. But these workers are nonetheless essential to Jobs's "do what you love" message, since they are the workers who helped facilitate his fantastic wealth. It is their work and the work of thousands of Apple's contract employees around the globe—from janitorial staff to cafeteria workers—that allow Jobs and the "professional" Apple employees to do *their* jobs. It is in large part because of their work that Jobs stood before his audience, soaking in the adulation as a public figure. It is true that the world's power wielders have always depended on the toil of nameless millions, who tilled fields, built cities, fought wars. Only recently, however, have these figures of the ruling class felt compelled to express love for the tasks of their own labor and to hold this love aloft as the key to their legitimacy as society's leaders.

The tendency to turn away from people we don't want to see manifests itself in everything from anti-loitering ordinances, meant to drive certain "undesirables" (teenagers, the homeless) from specific neighborhoods, to the US military's recently ended "Don't Ask, Don't Tell" policy, intended to keep its gay and lesbian workforce in the closet. Invisible workers tend to fall into two often-overlapping categories: workers whose labor either operates outside the work ethic or embodies the work ethic's broken promises. For instance, a significant amount of work in the service industry is self-evidently not performed "for its own sake." It's the work we pay people to do so we won't have to do it ourselves, like washing cars or stocking store shelves so that sundries remain at consumers' fingertips. The other large category of invisible work is work that, no matter how well or earnestly performed, fails to support a financially secure existence. When the quality and sincerity of work, say, as a call-center employee fails to deliver security and some measure of comfort, such work exposes the fraudulence of the idea that hard, earnest work guarantees a just reward. In order to maintain the belief that go-getterism really works, we must turn away from workers for whom it doesn't. While the tedious work of the world's masses might have been invisible simply because it was taken for granted, the rise of DWYL demands active refusal to acknowledge work that doesn't legitimize the ways in which the world's political, business, and social leaders justify their own power.

Lovable work is visible work. The question of who gets a public platform as a worker and who does not is neatly side-stepped by Jobs's narrative. What do those in the invisible workforce call themselves in their social media profiles? What kinds of identities are available to them?

These questions are critical because, as Jonathan Crary notes in his recent book, *24/7: Late Capitalism and the Ends of Sleep*, while the notion of identity is bound up with public visibility, today that public exposure has become detached from communal forms that once provided safekeeping and care.[1] Crary notes that in the always-on, 24/7 temporality in which we now live, the pressure to be constantly consuming or producing necessitates a constant presence in the public sphere, specifically in the marketplace. He writes, "No moment, place, or situation now exists in which one can *not* shop, consume, or exploit networked resources, there is a relentless incursion of the non-time of 24/7 into every aspect of social and personal life."[2]

Not only is having a public profile necessary for acknowledgment of one's very being, but also the marketplace has overwhelmingly become the venue for viewing and recognizing other individuals.[3] To be seen is to be seen from and within the market. "Do what you love" is a pretty accurate sorter for determining who is and isn't real or at least recognized. The DWYL professions just happen to be the ones that confer clout in the public realm. Whereas the manufacturing and industrial labor of the working class once garnered at least clichéd romanticism, the labor of today's working class, made up largely of low-wage service work, is utterly ignored. In *The New Yorker*, George Packer quipped, "No one composed a 'Ballad of the Floor Associate.'"[4]

Graduation speeches like Jobs's provide a tidy reflection of cultural values regarding work, but these speeches are seasonal and fleeting. Depictions of work created as popular entertainment, on the other hand, are with us year-round, constantly shaping expectations and values about the way laborers of all stripes conceptualize their own work. What images of work do audiences want to consume and what do they reveal about popular desires and assumptions about work? The workplace drama is a firmly established television genre with deep roots. I focus here on *The Good Wife* and *Enlightened*, and, later, on the documentary film *Finding Vivian Maier*, not only because they are relatively recent, but also because they directly address issues of visibility, worker identity, and gender.

By centering on white, middle-aged female protagonists coming to terms with their personas as workers, the very premises of these shows are linked to questions of the gendered politics of visibility within the entertainment industry itself. Although not unprecedented—*Murphy Brown* aired for the first time nearly thirty years ago—middle-aged female protagonists remain a somewhat unintuitive, if not provocative, choice for show runners. A common trope about middle-aged actresses is their post-ingenue–period obsolescence, and the fading middle-aged actress is its own cinematic motif, with Billy Wilder's *Sunset Boulevard* (1950) being perhaps the best-known example. But as cinema scholar Karen Beckman points out, the performance of vanishing is its own kind of spectacle, and no less a celebrity than Bette Davis embraced playing the role of the fading, middle-aged actress as part of her star persona.[5] Casting Juliana Margulies and Laura Dern, two beloved screen stars, as women negotiating drastic shifts in their own visibility cleverly demands that the viewers confront not whether but *how* we want to view middle-aged women, both as real-life celebrities and workers in fictional narratives.

By addressing popular depictions of middle-aged women at work here, we can focus tightly on the issue of visibility afforded by certain types of work through the lens of a demographic whose fading has been codified as simultaneously pathetic and spectacular. It is also a demographic that—it is assumed in the twenty-first century—has the ability to freely choose how to be visible as workers.

Specifically, both *The Good Wife* and *Enlightened* directly address the promise of self-actualization through work and the consequences of losing such work, respectively. In *The Good Wife*, Alicia Florrick (Margulies) returns to law practice after fifteen years as a wealthy stay-at-home mom. Her return is reluctant, necessitated by the imprisonment of her husband, former Illinois state's attorney Peter Florrick (Chris Noth), who was found guilty of corruption and soliciting prostitutes. The first season tracks Alicia's development from uncertain, lonely scandal collateral damage to an assertive, confident lawyer. *The Good Wife* pegs Alicia's personal development to her professional trajectory. Although Alicia is in her forties, by becoming a waged worker she is able to claim equal footing with her now-disgraced husband, command the respect of other professionals, and even make friends and form romantic attachments. It is Alicia's public role as a lawyer that provides her with access to these public *and* private relationships.

Several seasons in, Alicia's son, Zach (Graham Phillips),

tells her that he now views her as someone with an interior life apart from her role as a mother, as if the two are incompatible: "Sometimes I think of you as mom, and other times just as this interesting person who lives in our house." Alicia responds with a satisfied smile. Work also allows Alicia to put her strained marriage to work for her. By the fifth season, Peter has staged a political comeback and become the governor of Illinois. Long out of love with him, practical Alicia was never blind to the power that comes with being Peter's wife, even when he was imprisoned—something she savvily kept sight of when many others didn't.

Alicia's blossoming depends on the diametric opposition the show sets up between domestic and professional life. Yet the fact that both the show and its audience take it as a given that the office is a place of liberation and the home is one of obscurity and diminishment testifies to the triumph of a corporatist brand of feminism over some of the more radical possibilities proffered by international feminists in the 1970s. As we'll see, the tensions that the *The Good Wife* establish between domestic and professional spaces reinforces a highly specific iteration of feminism, one invested in professional achievement as a conduit to success, power, and visibility.

Although the show offers only fleeting flashbacks to Alicia's housewife past, it gives every indication that her life before the office was one of unreached potential. The professional Alicia appears to have maintained not one friend from her prework days and even confesses to a colleague that she can't imagine returning to her earlier life, having the conversations she used to. When asked whether she misses anything from her fifteen-year domestic interlude, Alicia describes the quiet afternoon hour before her children returned from school, when she'd sit alone, sipping a glass of wine. Alicia's recollection of these afternoons is wistful. On the one hand, this is a time in which Alicia is decidedly unproductive in her work as a mother and homemaker; on the other, an hour to spend alone, daydreaming in the quiet with a glass of wine, is an unequivocal luxury. But there is an ominous undertone to Alicia's quiet afternoons, as if savoring an hour with some Merlot is perhaps just a shade shy of descending into Betty Friedan's Valium-fogged "problem with no name." Both the frustrations and the pleasures of a purely domestic life are defined by blankness.

Alicia's "quiet hour" contrasts with the constant bustle of her work life. The show's episodes are frequently paced as countdowns or races against the clock, with Alicia and crew bolting in and out of courtrooms or scrambling to track down witnesses in order to beat some deadline, such as an execution or a filing date. In these episodes, Alicia is part of a proud tradition of can-do, kinetic film heroines, stretching back to the heyday of screwball comedy. The office is a place where the "exciting" Alicia can shine. In *The Good Wife*, Alicia possesses the quick wit and arch tongue of traditional screwball heroines, and puts them in the service of white-collar professionalism. Her work as a lawyer is what facilitates such freedom of movement, the ability to zip from office to courtroom to high-profile client's home to swanky holiday party, and to be seen as a person of consequence in these diverse locales.

The Good Wife does not outright assert that the office is the appropriate daytime dwelling for educated women of a certain class, but rather accepts this widely held assumption on the part of its audience. Yet such an opposition between office and home severely limits the liberating possibilities of each space: we see the home as hopelessly reactionary and the office, merely by the fact that it is not the home, as enlightened.

The show presents liberation and self-confidence as achievable through Alicia's capacity as a worker (though *The Good Wife* smartly complicates the Pollyanna-ish moral simplicity of "performing well at work": Alicia brandishes her husband's political stature and deceives colleagues to advance her career). The Wages for Housework movement of the '70s, by contrast, fought for public recognition for the work women were already doing in the home—cooking, cleaning, child rearing, elder care—work that facilitates the productivity and reproduction of waged workers, and upon which capitalism depends. Silvia Federici explicitly challenged the notion that the path to women's liberation cut through the office or factory. Why, when women were already spending their time performing emotionally and physically exhausting work, should a woman "go out and get a job so that you can join the struggles of the working class"? Understanding that for most women an executive-track career is not on the horizon, Federici asserted that "eight hours at a cash register or on an assembly line is hardly an enticing position proposition when you have to juggle it with a husband and kids at home."[6] Instead, she and others demanded greater visibility and financial remuneration for domestic work, as well as the right to a break from it. For them, the home could be a site of radical activism and a platform for public awareness. The dichotomy of the stifling home versus the liberating office presented in *The Good Wife* is but one of countless examples of how corporatized feminism has nudged more radical solutions out of the mainstream, and reflects contemporary expectations about and attitudes toward these two realms and those who occupy them.

Of course, generations of women have used the home as a space for organizing and power-wielding, and *The Good Wife* provides a model for this in the character of Jackie Florrick (Mary Beth Peil), Alicia's mother-in-law. Jackie is one of the show's chief villains, however, constantly meddling in her son's political maneuverings and resolutely disapproving of Alicia's return to work. Jackie is annoying because, unlike Alicia, she does not have a publicly sanctioned platform for exercising her influence. Because she is not a professional, she oversteps the bounds of her domestic sphere by persistently appearing in Peter's office and needling Alicia for her newfound ambitions.

The portrayal of professionalism that *The Good Wife* trades upon, moral compromises and all, is powerfully alluring. It's so attractive that the furniture company Mitchell Gold + Bob Williams offers a *Good Wife* line of furniture, featuring suites of home and office furnishings "belonging" to various characters on the show. For instance, "Alicia's Office Sofa," a mid-century-modern–inspired piece upholstered in corporate-sleek textured gray, retails for $2,195 and allows viewers the opportunity to bring the Alicia's aesthetic into their personal spaces. More than that, the sofa also offers its occupants a particularly intimate means of identification with the character: the physical connection of a shared seat, or even a way of inhabiting the character of Alicia Florrick herself.

"Alicia's Office Sofa" is a particularly canny item in the *Good Wife* furniture line because Alicia's office decoration functions as a big reveal in the fifth season. When Alicia is promoted, she's given a budget to redecorate her office; when the managing partner Diane Lockhart (Christine Baranski) realizes that Alicia's office is unchanged months later, it becomes a clue that Alicia is planning to bolt from the firm, taking some of its most lucrative clients with her. The new firm, in which Alicia is a founding partner and thereby proving she has come even more fully into her own, differs radically from her old one in . . . interior decor: an exposed-brick warehouse conversion with an open floor plan as opposed to genteel wood-paneled conference rooms. Bringing "Alicia's" office furniture into one's environment offers not only a physical vehicle for character identification, but also a way to experience a frisson of the show's narrative tensions. Other retailers have partnered with television shows—Banana Republic's *Mad Men* collection comes to mind—but the *Good Wife* furniture line stands out in the level of investment it demands, both financially and to the degree that these objects are incorporated into their owners' lives. These furnishings aren't high-end *Star Trek* costumes to be worn on occasion, but everyday items to be used over years, to the point where the connection to the show itself might even fade from consciousness. Nevertheless, the dramas and fantasies of the show are the furniture's key selling point.

The fantastical nature of *The Good Wife*'s portrayal of work is borne out by a recent investigation by the *New York Times* that finds that it is precisely at middle age that many professional women in America *leave* the workforce rather than enter it.[7] That is, women who have maintained active careers for a good two decades or so frequently leave the workforce during what would be their peak earning years in order to care for parents, children, and grandchildren. (Also, massive layoffs of government employees such as teachers have greatly affected women.)[8] Therefore, Alicia's spectacular reappearance in the public sphere as a professional, high-wage-earning worker after years in the home is precisely the opposite experience of a great many professional women.

Does this mean the show is selling its audience a bill of goods? Absolutely not. *The Good Wife* is, like any smartly written show, knowing and open about what it offers its viewers. It embraces its escapism. To enjoy a show that espouses the liberating and self-actualizing possibilities of waged work demands that its viewers approach it from a specific ideological standpoint—one in which identity is wedded to work and a person's public role. It demands that the audience find this story line, fantastical though it is, plausible as a narrative. The plausibility of this narrative rests largely on the kind of work Alicia does and her working conditions. Her initial search for work is premised upon her family's need for extra money. But unlike many women facing this challenge, Alicia doesn't become a greeter at a big-box store or a cafeteria worker. She becomes a worker whose unique skills and rhetorical talents have a public platform. She performs work that confers status upon her. And it is these *externally* bestowed laurels, determined by how she presents herself to the public, that give Alicia a sense of inner purpose, confidence to make friends and find romance, to negotiate the terms of her marriage—in short, a determined sense of identity lacking in the directionless housewife she had been.

The popularity of *The Good Wife*, then, provides a compelling view of what "ideal" work looks like to its audience. Sure, the days might be long, but work can soothe the disappointment of failed relationships, be a space for friendship, and, most important, bestow individuals with a claim to be seen and heard in the public sphere, which, in today's culture, means nothing less than having a claim to identity itself.

Alicia's inverse appeared on television screens in the form of Amy Jellicoe (Laura Dern), another middle-aged worker, shown sliding down her career ladder rather than hoisting herself up. The pilot episode opens with Amy in an office bathroom stall, in the midst of a rage attack. She returns to work after taking a leave of absence and spending time at a New Age rehabilitation retreat in Hawaii, determined not only to pick up where she left off professionally, but also to be a positive person deeply at peace with herself and the world—an "agent of change," in the parlance of her rehab center. On Amy's first day back at work, she meets with a human resources committee, who, unmoved by her professions of enthusiasm to be back at work, unceremoniously escorts her to the basement of the office tower of Abaddon Industries, the company that employs her. Quickly, Amy realizes that she will not be returning to her position as a buyer in the health and beauty department, but doing tedious data entry in seeming perpetuity. Before lunch on her first day back at work, Amy already feels all her hastily

learned and dearly paid-for positivity and sense of purpose slip-
ping through her fingers.

Stripped of the comforts of upper-middle management—
private office, windows, assistant—Amy toils in Abaddon's basement under fluorescent lights, at a desk in the middle of a large
room with nary a cubicle wall to shield her from her colleagues'
annoying tics and the constant surveillance of her obnoxious
manager, Dougie (Timm Sharp). Amy is given a startling lesson in the working conditions of Abaddon's employees that she
did not know existed. Not only has Amy been demoted, she
has started to vanish, literally buried out of view from her colleagues upstairs. Amy's public identity as an Abaddon executive
has been removed; when asked by her former, aboveground
colleagues what her new role is, she lies and tells them that
she's part of a cutting-edge project that will revolutionize the
company. The truth would only make explicit the stark division
from her former self and diminish her further in their eyes. *Enlightened* makes explicit this corporate hierarchy via repeated
shots of the headquarters' elevator, which functions as a sort-
ing apparatus; the status and respect—the visibility—afforded
to each worker is discernible simply by the floor-number but-
tons they push.

Even more sinisterly, Amy learns that her data-entry work is
part of an initiative to track the movements of Abaddon's warehouse workers—even less visible than the basement-bound

data-entry team—in order to reduce redundancies (i.e., facilitate layoffs). In other words, Amy's job is to dehumanize
the warehouse workers, reducing them to a series of tracked
movements, so that Abaddon can eliminate altogether as many
of them as possible and squeeze ever more productivity from
those who remain.

Initially clinging to her upper-management persona, Amy
refuses to see herself as one of the data-entry team. She fights
for her old role, claiming she doesn't belong in the basement—
she has too many ideas, she's too valuable. Over time, however,
as the finality of her demotion becomes clearer, she can't help
but befriend her desk neighbor, Tyler (Mike White), and comes
to see the data-entry team as individuals with their own ideas,
dreams, stresses, painful pasts. Amy's initial inability to "see"
her new colleagues speaks to the ways in which we're trained
to value certain types of work and overlook others.

Today's ideal worker is not the anonymous shift worker but
the enlightened genius who never stops working. Why respect
work that someone would want to *stop* doing at 5 p.m.? The pas-
sion-driven worker has work on the brain all the time (much to
the delight of his or her boss) and hence eagerly incorporates
this work into his or her identity. The work identity, in turn, confers prestige and recognition in the public forum. Shift work, on
the other hand, even white-collar shift work like data entry, is
work that is seen to demand no personal input from workers and

therefore provides no recognizable identity in the public arena. *Enlightened*'s Abaddon is representative of the American work-force as a whole in that the same self-validating jobs are the most respected, occupying the Parnassus of the office tower, even if they have little to do with the nuts-and-bolts manufacture and movement of the company's products.

Still, Amy struggles to find other avenues to be signifi-cant at Abaddon, to enact her new "agent of change" philos-ophy from rehab, itself an exhortation toward achieving and affirming visibility. Initially she tries to organize a women's group within the firm, a scheme everyone sees for what it is: a vehicle to raise Amy's own profile at work. It quickly fizzles. Later, another, better opportunity befalls Amy—she can be-come a whistle-blower. Her disrespect for boundaries (by turns hilarious and horrifying) pays off; her snooping leads her to discover some unsavory relationships Abaddon has with local politicians. She begins working with Jeff Flender (Dermot Mulroney), a well-known reporter, in order to deliver to him a scoop for the *Los Angeles Times*, a story that Amy imagines will center on her as the brave underdog heroine.

At one point, Jeff takes Amy to a reception organized around a photogenic librarian-activist's talk at a private multimillion-dollar home. The activist had organized some anti-corporate protests via Twitter; in the same episode, Amy joins Twitter for the same reason nearly every Twitter user does—to establish a public profile. Awed by the millionaires, CEOs, writers, and other globe-trotting "thought leader" types mingling amid the trays of catered refreshments as well as the librarian-activist's rapid rise in status, Amy later delivers an interior monologue: "I have joined the new world. I learn its language . . ." Quite rightly, Amy believes she has stepped into another realm, one in which rich, influential, and constantly flattered people (who naturally all happen to know and flatter one another) dwell, above and apart from even the consequential middle-manager class from which she has fallen, a world in which the right public profile can usher a librarian into the halls (or wine receptions) of power. At the party, Amy's be-dazzlement is ruptured by one of the catering staff, a young man who recognizes her as a regular patron of the chain restaurant where he also works. Humiliated, Amy rebuffs him, determined not to let a member of the servant class—whose job here is to be resolutely unnoticed—drag her into his orbit of invisibility when she's among so many people she wishes to impress.

At the reception, we see Amy struggling to negotiate her own visibility among an elite crowd of dignitaries. Her social status, along with everyone else's, is encoded in the party's network of gazes and recognitions: who sees whom and who is overlooked, whose gazes are welcome and whose aren't. It's an ecosystem in which wealth and occupational title are precious resources. Similar to the librarian-activist, Jeff draws a salary meager in comparison to many of the other guests' net worth, but his high-profile work grants him access to parties hosted by millionaires. Here, "journalist" and "activist" are officially interesting; "data entry" and "catering" are not. The latter two are tasks one performs, not identities in and of themselves. To fail to get the privileged types of work is to become invisible.

But what about the people who just don't care about being seen? The importance of public presence to our own self-conception becomes especially clear in our reactions to those who are entirely uninterested in establishing public profiles. To actively reject a public presence defined by self-commodification is utterly confounding. This confusion is everywhere in the documentary film *Finding Vivian Maier*, about a yet another middle-aged woman, a reclusive nanny who kept private her significant talent as a photographer. From the 1950s onward, Maier shot hundreds of thousands of rolls of film, capturing the daily experiences of her charges, life in the streets of Chicago, and nearly everything else in sight.

Her photographs and films, discovered posthumously in 2007 at a storage-unit auction, became wildly popular, drawing record attendance at galleries and worldwide recognition. But Maier herself remained a mystery. No one seemed to know anything about her life or why she chose to keep her work to herself. Throughout the film, several people who knew Maier, primarily the families for whom she worked, announce their astonishment that they lived in the midst of a talented artist.

More than once the interviewees ask hypothetically why Maier hid her work. "Why wouldn't you *share* it?" asks one, revealing how thoroughly Facebook parlance has co-opted the word *share* and affected subjectivity itself. If one makes something, naturally it must be "shared," that is, made public, commodified.

It becomes clear that Maier was aware of her artistic gifts, though she went to great lengths to keep them private, giving pseudonyms at the photo labs where she had her film developed and padlocking the rooms where she boarded. To the extent that she had a public presence, she chose to be seen by the world as a nanny. At one point, Maier wrote a letter to a photo developer in a remote village in France about possibly going into business together, although it is unclear whether she actually mailed it. She appears never to have made inquiries to major galleries or dealers about showing her photographs.

Maier's decision not to use her photographs as a means for public renown remains the central question of the film. Yet Maier's choice is only unintuitive when considered from a perspective that values public visibility above the work itself. As Rose Lichter-Marck writes in *The New Yorker*, "In the film, domestic work is placed in opposition to artistic ambition, as if the two are incompatible. But are they? Street photographers are often romanticized as mystical flâneurs, who inconspicuously capture *life qua life*, who are in the world, but not of it. The help, like the street photographer, is supposed to be invisible."[9] Maier seemed comfortable being "in the world, but not of it," and this quality of hers very possibly made both photography and domestic work appealing to her.

Her work as a nanny also afforded her the ability to practice her art in the way she preferred. One particularly clarifying event in the film is Maier's voyage around the world, which she paid for with wages she had saved. Alone, she traveled through Europe, South America, and Asia, photographing along the way. "Why would a nanny be taking all these pictures?" asks John Maloof, who discovered Maier's work, early in the film. The voyage makes clear that Maier was a nanny *so that* she could take her photographs. In many ways Maier remains an enigma despite the cataloging and minute inspection of her every remaining personal possession, the linguistic analysis of her affected European accent, the research of her genealogy. The incredulity at her choices and priorities, however, reveals much about ourselves.

Throughout the film, several of the speakers suggest or outright state that had Maier only made her work known, had she only walked through the doors of a downtown Chicago gallery, she would have been a famous art photographer. This belief says more about our own fantasies of success than it does about the realities of the art market. The fantasy is that the work, supposedly a labor of love—be it a photograph or an app—speaks for itself, that brilliance will shine through the slag heap. Such insistence that Maier's work would have made her famous if only it had been known betrays an intense faith in the correctness of our judgment as filtered through the free market—if only the work could have entered the market, we would have valued it the way we do now, that is, "properly," and surely Maier's own obscurity and apparently standoffish temperament would not have affected our aesthetic evaluation.

But every struggling artist knows that had Maier pursued galleries and dealers, there is no guarantee that she could have left nannydom, even if she wished to. Her lack of credentials and art world connections would certainly have been barriers to gaining gallery representation, let alone worldwide fame. Crafting an attractive persona in order to present one's creative work—artistic or otherwise—is also work, work that comes naturally and enjoyably to some, and less so to others. Among the fine arts, photography, especially, is widely practiced as a hobby. Many amateur photographers are indubitably very talented. No doubt there are scores of other undiscovered Maiers out there, who, for their own reasons, choose not to trade upon their work.

In *The Human Condition*, Hannah Arendt emphasizes that "a life spent entirely in public, in the presence of others, becomes, as we would say, shallow. While it retains its visibility, it loses the quality of rising into sight from some darker ground which must remain hidden if it is not to lose its depth in a very real, non-subjective sense."[10] Dwelling in this darker ground can be the "greatest forces of intimate life—the passions of the heart, the thoughts of the mind, the delights of the senses," all of which, compared to the glare of publicly affirmable reality, take on a shadowy quality, providing texture and dimensionality to life. The troubling reflection beaming back at us from *The Good Wife, Enlightened,* and *Finding Vivian Maier* is that self-fulfillment is something achieved through individuals' public activity, which in turn is largely defined by their waged work. To reject this paradigm of selfhood is to be not merely isolated (by choice or otherwise), but to be incomprehensible. Under this rubric it is unimaginable that the home could be a space of liberation or even radicalism, that a 9-to-5 data-entry job could be freeing in the leisure time it allows workers to fill, that artistic talent could be directed toward a kind of private, nonmonetized self-exploration.

For those raised with the expectation of creating a public identity, the necessity of constructing that profile is a matter of existential importance. This is more true now than before, as public activity is increasingly privileged over private matters. In *24/7*, Crary notes that even when we are most resolutely disengaged from the public sphere—when we are sleeping—our numerous social media profiles, "our patchwork of surrogate identities," now stand in as our waking avatars, projecting our photographs and opinions, receiving "likes" and comments.[11] Who is seen and unseen in this crowded, always-open agora hinges largely upon the type of waged work individuals perform and their ability to construct publicly visible identities out of that work.

That this reality is wrapped in the language of love and self-care through work demonstrates the extent to which identity itself has become conflated with the monetizable public profile. But what is lost when so much of life is dedicated to public display? In her essay about Facebook, Zadie Smith cautions that "those of us who turn in disgust from what we consider an over-inflated liberal-bourgeois sense of self should be careful what we wish for: our denuded networked selves don't look any more free, they just look more owned."[12] The pressure to peg our selves to our work and then present this conflated worker-self to the public in the most bland, nonideological, broadly consumable ways is limiting and disempowering. On a superficial level, it precludes dissent and opposition regarding our culture of work, but more fundamentally, dedicating so much time to surface presentation leaves little space for exploring the "darker ground" of private existence that Arendt speaks of. Even if Vivian Maier's professional "choices" seem bizarre, or at least at odds with mainstream values, never in her self-portraits does she look owned.

2

—

THE MIRAGE
of AUTONOMY

I want to claw my way to middle management.

—Monster.com commercial (2010)

If you have to control people, you have to have an administrative force that does it. So in US industry even more than elsewhere, there's layer after layer of management—a kind of economic waste, but useful for control and domination.

—Noam Chomsky, "The Death of American Universities" (2014)[1]

In July 2014, journalist Ryan Block wished to cancel a Comcast cable service account over the telephone. Several minutes in, and exasperated at his inability to complete a seemingly straightforward transaction, Block began recording the call. He taped eight additional minutes of his excruciating exchange with a Comcast customer service representative and posted it on SoundCloud. The dialogue between Block and the representative is a loop of despair: Block asking for service cancellation, the representative asking for a reason for the cancellation, Block declining to provide one and reiterating his request, and the representative rephrasing the question of why. Clearly, frustrating experiences with customer service calls are not unique to Block, and the unnamed representative quickly became the Internet's villain du jour. The mass disgust with the representative was not surprising. As the public instinctively knows, customer service is only partially about service. Additionally, when typically invisible service economy workers do improbably emerge in popular media, they're often figures of scorn or ridicule. And no wonder—relying largely on tips, commissions, and other per-transaction financial incentives instead of steady salaries, these workers not only provide a specific service but have become the people onto whom we can cathartically unload our lives' frustrations. Telling off a "mindless" service worker is its own cultural trope; in popular reception, Block's Comcast rep comes from the same lineage as the "stupid" waitress in *Five Easy Pieces* who won't take an order for an item not offered on the menu. Why wouldn't the waitress just serve up some toast, and why wouldn't the representative just give Block some "quality assurance" and cancel the cable service already?

Because the *Five Easy Pieces* waitress was right: she doesn't make the rules. The Comcast rep was likely being surveilled while doing his job, which is primarily to earn revenue for Comcast, or, at least, keep the company from losing it. Perhaps the representative's relentless requests for a reason behind the desired cancellation were the petty cruelties of a deranged individual. More likely, however, they were increasingly desperate attempts to pivot the transaction away from a cancellation. In the wake of the publicity from Block's call, a former Comcast employee told *Businessweek* that while Comcast didn't impose a script for service calls, the company did require representatives to enter a reason for account cancellations. There were also financial inducements for representatives to keep customers from canceling service or to upgrade their subscriptions. For every service call, representatives had a series of questions to answer on their computer systems, effectively slowing down the conversation (and accounting for the stilted dialogue of customer service calls in general). Notably, the former Comcast representative stated, "I always felt really disempowered to do the right thing." She continued, "They didn't care about the hours you had to work or whether or not their policies made sense for you in their job."[2]

Restricted by several methods of surveillance and control, the Comcast representative was in fact unable to engage Block in a human conversation that was fully considerate of his needs and wishes—a condition Block himself acknowledged when interviewed later about the call. As John Herrman put it succinctly in *The Awl*, "The rep didn't abuse Block, and Block didn't torture the rep. Comcast, the organization, is tormenting them both."[3]

In no way do I wish to romanticize the mental and emotional exhaustion of fielding customer service calls all day, but what if the Comcast representative might actually *want* to like his job (as a service provider, not a salesman in the guise of a service provider)? What if service representatives could actually feel unencumbered in addressing their customers' needs and therefore derive satisfaction from helping people? This possibility is thwarted by the fact that true autonomy is something that barely exists in today's workplace. Instead, phalanxes of managers, administrators, and "experts" are installed to oversee workforces in the belief that workers are incapable of doing their jobs without constant administrative observation and evaluation. As we shall see, one of the primary functions of this managerial apparatus is to apply persistent pressure on workers to align even their most personal desires, regarding everything from their hobbies to care of their own bodies, with their employers'. DWYL rhetoric plays a large part in this project.

AUTONOMY VS. SURVEILLANCE

Of course, effective management is essential not only to the day-to-day functioning of a workplace, but also in eliciting positive feelings about work: satisfaction deriving from collaboration and teamwork, security that a workplace is safe and harassment-free, assuredness in clear communication. Things start to go awry when everyone from maids to CEOs are under pressure to present as "passionate" workers, especially during the present era of increasing financial insecurity. Under these conditions, the burden on management to align the personal desires of workers with their employers' aims—always a tricky endeavor—grows heavy. The work of reconciling these potentially, perhaps naturally, divergent desires comprises a miscellany of disciplinary techniques, nearly all of which begin with surveillance. Worker surveillance is the beginning point (and sometimes the omega as well) of nearly all managerial activity, and today workers are being surveilled more extensively than ever before.

Workers everywhere, from call centers to restaurants to warehouses, have their every transaction and sometimes their every movement recorded by various devices. So-called digital sentinels are in use in thousands of restaurants across the United States, recording individual servers' every ticket, dish, and drink served. Tech companies are racing to develop even more intrusive monitoring systems, including a "sociometric badge" equipped with a microphone and an accelerometer, capable of recording an employee's "tone of voice, posture, and body language, as well as who spoke to whom and for how long."[4] Dr. Ben Warber, whose company issues the sociometric badges and analyzes the data they generate, stresses that his company operates on a strictly opt-in basis and only delivers aggregate data to the companies with which it contracts: "You can't see, 'Where is Bob at 2:30 on Tuesdays?' There's no good business case for why you need that data."[5] Yet with this technology (and its in-depth analysis) still in its early stages, Warber nonetheless adds that he believes that formal, legal protections regarding this kind of intensive data collection on workers are necessary: "In the U.S., especially, it's the Wild West around people-analytics data."[6] Lest anyone think that such meticulous monitoring is something foisted only on low-wage and service workers, the badge has garnered interest from companies in the banking, pharmaceutical, and health-care industries.[7]

Fundamentally, such monitoring technology is aimed at managing the social interactions of workers, so that it can be harnessed to generate value,[8] but it also nudges workers into specific social situations management deems advantageous to its bottom line. Like any extension of management, it can cut both ways and success hinges on the sensitivity with which it's implemented. Through employee monitoring, one call center found that tight-knit work groups recorded greater productivity and reduced turnover. The center introduced 15-minute coffee breaks into the daily routine to encourage social communication, resulting in 10 percent greater productivity and an impressive 70 percent drop in turnover.[9] Broadly considered, the call center's case is a clear success, but on the individual level it's easy to imagine such breaks being stressful for someone who is otherwise competent but feels he doesn't fit in, or one toxic personality turning the breaks into something less than rejuvenating. Peter Cappelli, director of the Center for Human Resources at the University of Pennsylvania's Wharton School of Business, cautions that while workplace analytics is being presented as a supposedly objective and progressive development liberating workers from the irrational whims of managers, the same was said of scientific industrial management in the 1920s, in which workers' every movement was recorded against a stopwatch—and that scientific management eventually became a "speed-up dogma" that workers found oppressive.[10]

No likes being surveilled. Even workers in the national

security surveillance business resist managerial surveillance of their own work. This is true *even though surveillance would materially improve the quality of their work*, work they are doing perhaps out of some sense of patriotic duty (a specific form of love). Prior to the Edward Snowden leak, the US National Security Agency (NSA) possessed employee-monitoring technology that would have detected Snowden copying sensitive material before he leaked it, something his institution and, ostensibly, his colleagues would wish to prevent. This technology was not put to use, however, because NSA workers themselves protested the idea of being so closely watched by higher-ups.[11] In other words, spies working in the interest of national security resisted their own surveillance even at the risk of the national security in which they were ideologically invested.

The promise of worker autonomy is embedded in the "you" of DWYL. Worker autonomy is a broadly appealing idea because it isn't limited to any particular kind of work. Whether a job engages an individual's unique intellect or consists primarily of physical labor, the potential to derive satisfaction from it often lies in the worker's sense of self-determination in doing it. It is the application of individual skills along with the recognition of them (especially in the form of wages) that underlies a sense of accomplishment.

And yet how free can workers possibly be? How did the highly specific and unintuitive idea of enjoying work even come about? Economist Frédéric Lordon analyzes the uncomfortable answers to these questions. Lordon articulates the general truth that those of us who labor are compelled to do so according to a carrot-and-stick apparatus of negative consequences and positive striving (though, for each worker, the proportion of these motivations will be unique). On the negative end, we work under the threat of hunger. On the positive end, we work in order to obtain the things we desire, both abstract and material: admiration of the community, as well as consumable products. From the perspective of employers, who desire employees' complete absorption in their work, Lordon efficiently identifies the problem of the carrot-and-stick model in that it is both negative and external to the work itself: "The spur of hunger is intrinsic to employment, but it is a sad affect. Consumerist joy is indeed a joyful affect, but it is an extrinsic one." The ruthless neoliberal project, according to Lordon, is to construct a model of work that produces "intrinsic joyful affects." In other words, it encourages the reimagining of work as a source of joy in and of itself. Once work becomes its own reward in the eyes of the worker, it completely obliterates the threat of hunger (the sad affect) from his consciousness and becomes not a *means* to external pleasures (the positive but extrinsic affect), but the very source of joy.[12]

It makes complete sense that DWYL tropes circulate wildly at the same time workers are more closely surveilled and more heavily managed than ever before. Surveillance allows managers and business owners to unceasingly monitor the workers' desires so they might better bring them in line with what the company requires. If a warehouse worker wants to avoid an unpleasant colleague in a certain row, a tracking device notes his deviation from the route predetermined to be the most efficient and delivers this data to software processed by workers like Amy Jellicoe in *Enlightened*. If the warehouse worker's lunch didn't agree with him, the tracking device notes the uptick in his bathroom breaks. He will then have to explain these unorthodox warehouse routes to management, just as customer service representatives must account for deviant questionnaire answers. Thus does this surveillance affect the hypothetical worker's desires—the desires to avoid a colleague or attend to his own physical comfort may be diminished by the countervailing desire to avoid managerial censure.

The drive to align employees' desires and values with their employers' does not stop when the work does. Management has many tools at hand to affect how workers spend their non-working hours. While working at Lululemon, the retailer of pricey yoga gear, writer Mary Mann received a company-paid membership at a high-end Manhattan yoga studio that, she acknowledges, she wouldn't have been able to afford if the membership fee amount had simply been included in her paycheck. (Rent and other basics would have absorbed the extra money.)

The gym membership was part of Lululemon's effort to make its salespeople (or "educators," in company parlance) seem like they belonged to the world of its customers, even though for Mann, "it wasn't part of a world I wanted."

Other off-the-clock intrusions are more severe. Fashion models are frequently paid in trade (with clothes and products), which not only spares employers from paying them actual money, but also encourages models to don a brand's wares after work and without an endorsement fee. Perhaps most intrusive is the recent US Supreme Court decision in favor of the retail chain Hobby Lobby. The court declared that the company's health-care plan, to which employees contribute their earnings, need not cover certain forms of contraception. In other words, if workers opt into Hobby Lobby's health-care plan (hardly a choice for most workers), the company can determine how its workers may dispense their wages.

RISE OF THE MANAGERS

As colleges and universities churn out more and more would-be professionals, it is becoming clear to this class of workers that autonomy is an empty promise. This expansion and simultaneous enfeeblement of the professional class is curious. When a group grows in size, we may intuitively expect it to grow more powerful, but precisely the opposite is happening with professional workers, and these developments are radically changing the way we conceive of class and social mobility. While de-skilling in manufacturing once worked to make existence *within* the working class more disempowered, today it unleashes the same precariousness of existence on professional workers.

The DWYL ethos promotes a denial of class politics that is both insistent and seemingly guileless. Polite society may prefer to pretend otherwise, but the kind of jobs that provide public visibility, ready-made identities, and the promise of self-fulfillment are strictly cordoned off by class boundaries. The rhetorical sleight of hand achieved by conceits of work-for-love is the elision of wages—and, hence, class—from discourses of labor. DWYL provides cover for beguiling ourselves that work and class float free from each other, that the type of work one does is a function of personal choice rather than class membership, and that class membership is a function of nebulous other factors, often implying strength (or frailty) of moral character. Of course, the reality is that today more than ever, at least in the United States, the class into which one is born overwhelmingly determines the kind of work an individual will perform throughout his or her life.

In 1977, Barbara and John Ehrenreich laid out a historically informed description of what they call the professional-managerial class (PMC). The twentieth century's growing ranks of professors, engineers, managers—were they really "working class" merely by dint of not owning the means of production (e.g., the factories, libraries, offices they used to produce their work)? No, argue the Ehrenreichs; they constitute a separate class, the PMC, with singular interests apart from (and often antagonistic to) both labor and capital. In their own words:

> We define the Professional-Managerial Class as consisting of salaried mental workers who do not own the means of production and whose major function in the social division of labor may be described broadly as the reproduction of capitalist culture and capitalist class relations.[13]

The PMC consists of experts with direct control over the working class (managers, engineers) as well as those who shape class ideology in the broader culture (advertising executives, professors). While not of the capitalist (ownership) class, the PMC nonetheless exists as a force both ideological and physical that reinforces class relations under capitalism. The PMC is therefore, fundamentally, a disciplining class that serves to maintain a specific form of social order.

In the United States, they argue, the PMC emerged with sudden breadth during the Progressive Era (c. 1890–1920).[14] Although historicized as a period that brought many of the worst capitalist abuses to heel, the Progressive Era also greatly expanded a class of workers whose essential function is to monitor and control other workers both directly (in the workplace) and indirectly (via educational, social, and cultural institutions), a legacy that lasts to this day. Whereas in the nineteenth century the owners of capital were largely left to hire enforcers whose main tool against worker discontent was reactive violence, managers could exert more constant, direct, and pervasive control over workers by assuming hierarchical positions in the workplace and in popular culture.[15]

It was during this period that the first business schools and journals appeared alongside the discipline of management theory and management gurus such as Frederick Winslow Taylor (1856–1919).[16] Under Taylor's management rubric, known commonly as Taylorism, teams of overseers constantly monitored workers to ensure that their division of labor, individual movements, and rest periods were ceaselessly refined to maximize efficiency of production.[17] Essentially, Taylorist "scientific rationalization" of work renders complex processes into separate, simple, repetitive motions or transactions and fundamentally undermines the key source of workers' power: craft knowledge.[18] The PMC claimed expertise of work flows and production from the workers themselves without ever having been part of the working class. As we shall see, the co-opting of expertise away from workers continues to have profound consequences for a growing roster of professions.

Today, the PMC is pulled in two directions. As the labels of PMC professionalism, the empty accoutrements of worker autonomy, trickle down—secretaries are now called "administrative assistants," cashiers called "associates"—the perks of membership (pensions, noncontingency, comfortable wages) are eroding. In fact, in 2013, the Ehrenreichs issued an update to their original paper, chronicling the ruthless re-assertion of the capitalist class over the PMC since the 1970s. Massive downsizing and exporting of working-class jobs left mid-level managers with no one to manage. Government cuts slashed teaching and research jobs. "Unemployed and underemployed professional workers—from IT to journalism, academia, even law—became a regular feature on the social landscape."[19] In effect, the professional class has been cannibalizing itself. In the last several decades, numerous sectors of professional work have become targets for de-skilling, including teaching both at the primary-school and university levels, journalism, and law, among others.

MANAGED TEACHING AND LEARNING

A kindergartner sits, isolated from her classmates by a "privacy board," filling out worksheets for a large part of the school day. Sheets with incorrect answers are sent home with the tot to be redone in addition to the regular hour of homework. While this scenario might seem like it belongs in a farcical movie parodying the excesses of some state communist regime east of the Iron Curtain, it is in fact how one Arizona mother described her daughter's school experience to *Washington Post* education reporter Valerie Strauss in 2014.[20] The reason children as young as five and barely able to grasp pencils spend hours silently puzzling over worksheets instead of building block towers together or exploring local wildlife is that they are preparing for standardized tests by which they, their school, and their teachers will be ranked.

If it intuitively strikes you as wrong that the youngest schoolchildren should be measured and managed with obsessive data-gathering techniques borrowed from the worlds of business, marketing, and mass-production manuals,[21] a significant body of research on early-childhood education bears you out, indicating that standardized testing is age-inappropriate for young children, especially those under eight years, and that the results it produces are unreliable.[22] For instance, the National Association of School Psychologists stated in a 2005 position paper that "evidence from research and practice in early childhood assessment indicates that issues of technical adequacy are more difficult to address with young children who have little test-taking experience, short attention spans, and whose development is rapid and variable."[23] As early as 1987, the National Association for the Education of Young Children (NAEYC) discouraged rigorous testing of children under age eight, instead advocating for a more holistic assessment involving teacher observation and work portfolios.[24] And yet intensive testing of young children continues apace, typically in the name of school or education reform.

So-called school reform came to the fore in the United States with a report spearheaded by Terrel Bell, secretary of education under President Reagan: *A Nation at Risk: The Imperative for Educational Reform*, which characterized America's schools as mediocre to the point of damaging national economic security.[25] The report helped launch a relentless parade of technocratic programs that have been inflicted upon public schools in order to reform them. After decades of school reform schemes, many of which have enriched investors eager to sop up some of the trillions of dollars the government spends on public education, America is still rife with underfunded schools unable to meet their communities' needs. What has changed under decades of reform schemes are the conditions under which teachers work, as well as very nature of teaching.

One of the biggest changes has been the introduction of high-stakes standardized testing, which pits schools against one another for government funding, and even for their continued existence. Depending on the district, schools with low scores are shuttered and sometimes replaced with charter schools, which receive taxpayer money but are accountable to private managers. Scores are also used to shame teachers, districts, and even children themselves: at the city's annual convocation ceremony, Atlanta schoolchildren are seated either on the field or in the stands of the Georgia Dome depending on their school's test scores;[26] a district in Massachusetts required teachers to post students' scores—with their full names—on "data walls" in the hallways of an elementary school.[27] While such ranking tactics are hardly new, today they speak to the frenzied sense of competition and insecurity pervading schools made to compete constantly with one another for dwindling resources.

With teachers and districts no longer deemed qualified to evaluate their own students or give their professional opinions about their school's needs (namely funding, the one thing they are consistently denied), standardized testing corporations are only too happy to swoop in and declare their products the appropriate metrics by which student progress can be measured. Originally an open-ended process of intellectual stewardship, teaching has become a manufacturing process with an easily measured end product: test scores.[28] With the teaching profession thus Taylorized,[29] teachers themselves become deskilled workers, and more darkly, students are first and foremost the means of generating data, and then, only as a second thought, can schools consider them as blossoming individuals. The data, in turn, are used to threaten teachers with shame and termination.

One of the most disheartening developments brought about by high-stakes testing is the proliferation of cheating scandals it has triggered across the country. Naturally, teachers, principals, and other administrators are desperate to keep their jobs, particularly in today's weak labor market in which layoffs in public education are especially rampant. Many involved in the cheating scandals—cases in which teachers and administrators correct student answers before the exams are scored—are tormented by their deeds, borne out of desperation to maintain their livelihoods, as well as to keep beloved community schools from being shuttered. One Atlanta teacher who changed scores recalls being unable to look a colleague in the eye, so great was his disbelief at what they were doing.[30] The widespread cheating is appalling, but it shouldn't be surprising. Whenever institutions are subjected to superficial accountability measures without being given actual resources to address deep-seated problems, fraud nearly always follows suit.

Other depressing aspects of high-stakes testing are its superficiality and the massive amount of waste it produces. Teachers devote significant amounts of classroom time to test preparation and drills, despite the fact that these tests provide only an extremely limited, one-dimensional understanding of what unfolds in a classroom, and are an extremely narrow metric by which to evaluate the intellectual development of a human being. An ESL student may improve his or her English verbal skills by leaps and bounds in a given school year but still test below native speakers. The student's improvement and the teacher's success thus show up as failures. Perhaps most scandalously, many schools administer pilot versions of standardized tests during school hours—these tests exist not to evaluate students or teachers, but solely to provide feedback to for-profit testing companies on the utility of prospective questions on future exams. In other words, class time is taken from students and teachers, and children are essentially performing unpaid labor as research and development test subjects.[31] The disparity between the tests' utility and profitability clarifies the true motivations behind high-stakes testing. Standardized tests do a poor job of holistically evaluating students, yet the private testing and scoring companies that sell their services and wares to public schools generate hundreds of millions of dollars in revenue.[32] High-stakes testing works to disempower public sector workers and wastes significant amounts of students' and teachers' time in the name of profit for private companies.

Surely there needs to be a way to evaluate students and schools, but other countries manage this without obsessive testing. Finland, in which schools "even" in immigrant and working-class districts manage to produce university- and workforce-ready individuals competent in three languages (Finnish, Swedish, and English), does not mandate testing but leaves it optional except for one exam at the end of high school.[33] A host of other social and cultural factors underpin Finland's educational success; primary-school teaching is a well-compensated and competitive profession for which top university students compete, and social welfare programs ensure that students generally do not show up at school hungry or homeless.[34] Rather than competing against one another for raises (or their very jobs), Finnish teachers are empowered to collaborate when faced with challenges such as a non-Finnish-speaking student or a child with special needs.[35]

The expansion of standardized testing in the United States is only one of many neoliberal gimmicks aimed at de-skilling the teaching profession in the name of reform. While tarring experienced, unionized teachers as lazy, reformers tout inexperienced, cursorily trained teachers as a force that will shake up the classroom. Challenges to teacher tenure are making their way through California courts. Instead of developing their own curricula and engaging in spontaneous interaction with students, many teachers must now read scripted lesson plans to their students.

"David," a teacher with nearly a decade of experience in the Philadelphia public schools, characterizes the market-based reform schemes as punitive for both teachers and communities. According to him, the discipline is driven by elitism and comes down largely along class lines. Belief that a Teach for America recruit, trained for only a few weeks but most likely bearing an elite degree, will be a more effective teacher than someone with years of experience is a move to discipline professional teachers and poor communities themselves. Test scores determine not only which teachers are retained and which are fired, but also—proving the Ehrenreichs' point—determine in part which students are admitted to the best magnet schools and which districts get resources (usually the rich ones), thus reinforcing and reproducing class structures already in place.

Neoliberal education reform rationalizes the rich and complex craft of primary-school teaching into something that can be measured according to manager-determined rubrics. In the name of accountability, standardized-testing corporations, test-prep corporations, and an apparatus of reformer-managers feed on the teaching profession, inserting layers of bureaucracy staffed by many who have never taught or who have done so only briefly. Teachers are hardly alone; the field of journalism, although it often entails expensive credentials (a bachelor's degree and occasionally a master's), presents many entering the field with a menu of unpaid or low-paid, nonpermanent internships and fellowships. At the same time, news outlets happily reprint blog posts written by nonprofessionals for free and mine Twitter for exchanges to aggregate on their Web pages. Some newspapers have practically eliminated photojournalists—why pay trained photographers when every reporter has a camera on his or her phone? Even the exalted medical profession has long ceased to be a haven from de-skilling, with health-insurance and hospital administrators wedging their way into doctor-patient relationships by having a say over treatments.

Although these developments have been unfolding for decades, resistance has come largely through angry mutterings rather than collective action. Professional workers have traditionally been allergic to mass protest. Striking and openly making demands for workers' rights have never been part of the professional class's DNA—such tactics are typically employed by the working class; in fact, they are part of what defines it as a class. Moreover, such action would mean openly turning on members of their own class. One of the hallmarks of the professional class is the ability to rise within it—when workers think they have a chance of earning a promotion to their bosses' jobs, open confrontation makes little sense for them. As Nikil Saval points out in his history of the modern office, the nineteenth-century clerk, prototype of the modern midlevel company accountant, was more inclined to appeal to his boss's goodwill when he had a working-condition demand than to organize a strike.[36] Today, professional workers only redouble their efforts to show their bosses and announce to the world how happy and grateful they are for their work. "Love my job!" is the leitmotif on corporate Instagram accounts, frequently administered by low-paid (typically female) interns or public relations staffers. Luckily for employers, the popular culture of insistent happiness codified by DWYL provides an efficient way for workers to outwardly and insistently project how thrilled they are to be working.

That the teaching profession has been targeted for de-skilling through increased managerial control is unsurprising. Teachers are hardly alone as targets of de-professionalizing policies. But why are policies aimed at teachers so numerous and so vehement? To begin with, teachers stand out from the rest of the professional class in that they are female majority and broadly unionized. David offers a compelling list of additional reasons. Traditionally, teachers are specialized workers whose work entails and encourages freedom of thought. Furthermore, their schedules allow for time to "pursue outside interests, to organize, write op-eds." A significant reason why teaching had been such an appealing job for many is that at one point, the desires of teachers and the communities in which they taught (their employers) were naturally similar, even if not always completely aligned. Freedom of thought and time to nurture outside interests foster a less standardized kind of teaching, one in which teachers are more able to respond to students' individual needs and interests. Each of the qualities mentioned by David represents a potentially drastic drift from employers' desires and agendas when those employers are no longer local communities but manager-reformers invested in the constant raising of test scores.

Also at issue is the role gender plays in DWYL tropes and the emotional nature of any work involving the care of children. Teaching, particularly to young children, is traditionally gendered female, and female-gendered work is often assumed to be done out of love. (Women are nurturers, and not so crass as to demand money for helping.) When teachers join a union or make demands regarding pay and working conditions, these actions make explicit their status as workers as opposed to altruistic caregivers. Most teachers genuinely like their pupils. But perhaps the uncomfortable truth is, outside of homeschooling, exceedingly few people are going to teach children multiplication tables or how to write five-paragraph essays for free. Nor should they have to; as with all workers, teachers' dedication to, and love of, their profession is not contradictory to their assertion of rights as workers.

THE LABOR OF MANAGING

As for the managers themselves, what are they doing all day? Waiting for it to end, according to Carl Cederström and Paul Fleming in their book, *Dead Man Working*. "From the daily tedium of the office, to the humiliating team building exercise, to the alienating rituals of the service economy, to the petty mind games of the passive-aggressive boss: the experience is not one of dying . . . but neither of living."[37] Cederström and Fleming argue that for the majority of workers, the end of work is what they are working for: the end of a shift, the end of a career, even the end of life itself. The aim of so-called corporate cultures is to distract workers from this bleak reality, through canned fun in the form of office games, motivational speaking, and retreats. These schemes are not necessarily productive but are effective for social control.

Benjamin Ginsburg, a political scientist at John Hopkins University, is slightly less dreary, describing much of administrative work as "make-work": a merry-go-round of scheduling meetings, going to meetings, staff retreats, and "strategic planning." Citing the minutes of several administrative meetings on different university campuses, Ginsberg concludes, "These examples conjure up a nightmarish vision of administrative life in which staffers and managers spend much of the day meeting to discuss meetings where other meetings are discussed at which still other meetings have been discussed. This vision may seem bizarre, but unfortunately it is not far from the truth."[38] At one "President's Staff Meeting," eleven of the eighteen agenda items involved planning future meetings or discussions of previously held meetings.[39] Looking at meeting minutes and strategic plans, he observes that the resolved items are typically trivial ("give final examinations only during the final examination period"[40]) or almost comically vague (recommend the creation of a "Culture Committee. . . . Since culture is a notoriously abstruse issue, this committee may need to meet for years, if not decades, to unravel its complexities"[41]). One thing that this parade of meetings does accomplish, Ginsburg notes, is the continued mushrooming of administrators on campuses. The straightforward goals sprinkled among the nebulous or redundant resolved items frequently include plans to hire more administrators. Several months or years after a meeting or unveiling of a strategic plan, the hiring of additional administrators are some of the only things on these to-do lists that are actually accomplished.[42]

In one instance, Ginsburg recalls an administrator informing him that he would join Ginsburg in running an undergraduate academic program to which Ginsburg had been happily tending on his own.[43] According to Ginsburg, this administrator was trying to make work for himself that was technically unnecessary, while at the same time trying to undermine the authority of a university professor—a worker who actually carries out the teaching and research missions of the university that employs them both. And yet asserting managerial control over other workers and encroaching upon their craft knowledge, it seems, isn't exactly lovable work. According to a 2013 Gallup study, "State of the American Workplace," managers and executives, while more "engaged" at work than heavily managed transportation and service workers, were hardly the picture of bliss. Over half of them fell into the categories "not engaged" and "actively disengaged."[44] The frustrations experienced by Ginsburg and his colleagues aren't necessarily the machinations of a malicious individual; rather, they exemplify the ways in which managerial structures take on a life of their own through frenetic self-validation, inventing work for people that doesn't actually need to be done.

Ginsburg takes care to acknowledge that he speaks broadly, and not about every manager and administrator personally. He names several university officials who, he feels, have done admirable work in keeping complex institutions running smoothly. It's also important not to get too nostalgic for the days before certain administrative inputs, when the professoriat kept academia largely white and male. Indeed, there are scores of managers laboring in offices and cubicles who do produce tangible work to the benefit of their colleagues and the greater community. The problem is, there are far more administrators than administrative work, and extraneous workers are left to rely on the trappings of professionalism—titles, authority, particularly the office—to provide cover for make-work.

Jenny Diski observes that the white-collar office has always been a space defined by what *doesn't* happen there. People work in offices, but "there's no real clue as to what they do, unlike people who work in other places, who make things in a factory, mine things in a mine, teach in school, sell things in a shop."[45] Rather, the office is a containment space for all kinds of fetish-worthy objects: crisp letterhead, pushpins, rubber stamps, each in its own dedicated and precisely located container, waiting to be used.[46] The pleasure of management, manifested in part by these material totems, largely derives from power relations vis-à-vis the managed. "The manager is the very model for the kind of happy worker capitalism would like to create," writes Lordon. For, while they, too, toil underneath the ruling class, they do so cheerfully due to the few scraps begrudged them that separate them from the working class: a steady salary as opposed to hourly or piece-rate wages, a modicum of control over other workers allowing them to feel "symbolically on the side of capital,"[47] and, of course, offices, those tiny, individual throne rooms.

Today, many of these perks are long gone, the company pension and the typewriter ribbon both on the verge of extinction. Only the vagueness of office work survives, without many of its ameliorating comforts. It's hardly surprising that fewer than half of American managers and executives are "engaged" and less surprising still that they're not exactly beacons of inspiration to those they manage.

The fantasy of visible professional-managerial work, such as that projected in *The Good Wife*, is that this work is fulfilling and invigorating. But the recent economic crisis and feeble recovery have exposed much of it as largely useless, or at least redundant. The massive layoffs within the high-end law industry reveal that many of those posts were in fact make-work. Less flush with cash, many of these firms' clients have decided that the work they were purchasing wasn't actually worth as much after all.

Of course, many workers actively do try to avoid the surveillance and discipline of management altogether. In fact, the DWYL dream supports this wholeheartedly. What could be a greater gift to oneself than self-employment, the true source of worker autonomy? To refuse the surveillance and discipline of managers, to work in honor of one's unique visions, to forgo the PMC in favor of individual practice, or, better yet, to leap directly into the capital class via entrepreneurship—such is the path forged by the likes of Mark Zuckerberg and Bill Gates. It is because of their self-determination and status as visionaries (both left Harvard to chase their individual destinies, or so the mythology goes) as much as their extreme wealth that they stand as cultural icons.

And yet, for most, the reality of self-employment, entrepreneurship, and freelance work exacts a high cost. Most obviously, without a large, continuous contract, the income is anything but steady, making any kind of long-term planning (home buying, retirement planning) nearly impossible. Furthermore in the United States, flying solo means forgoing premium employee-sponsored health insurance, employee-matching retirement savings accounts, and paid sick leave or vacation time.

All too often, refusing the surveillance and discipline of

working for another means embracing a precarious life—patching together odd jobs as they come, hoping to eke out enough income to cover living expenses. Many of the jobs in the so-called gig economy, such as yoga instruction and freelance writing, bear the veneer of pleasure, of earning money while doing enjoyable things. Kept offstage from the vision of flexible schedules and sunlit studios is the grueling unpaid work that goes into facilitating these careers: pitching articles and books (and racking up rejections), tracking down delinquent clients, constantly marketing one's services. For most freelancers, these efforts barely pay off.[48] According to labor economist Gerald Friedman, "The gig economy is associated with low wages, repression, insecurity, and chronic stress and anxiety."[49]

Questions of professionalism, class anxiety, the imagined ideal of worker autonomy, and love are coming to a head at the present moment. Many people feel there's something wrong with themselves if they don't enjoy their work or can't find work they love. Professionalism presented one pathway toward "fulfilling" work, but many such jobs are becoming deprofessionalized or disappearing altogether. In different ways, Cederström and Fleming, Gallup, and Ginsburg have shown that many find the labor of the white-collar manager alienating and empty in any case. For the first time since the bachelor's degree became a middle-class expectation, a significant number of would-be professionals find themselves in the low-wage service economy, at least for a time, like Aaron Braun and Mary Mann. If the good middle-class jobs really are disappearing, perhaps it's time to acknowledge what all the rhetoric about love and autonomy was always about.

DWYL distracts workers with visions of nonexistent autonomy and vague self-fulfillment while persuading them to assume capital's interests as their own. That it shares an orbit with professionalization, management, and class anxiety is not coincidental. Just like each of these, DWYL is, fundamentally, a form of social control.

3

TIERED WORK SYSTEMS and the LABOR of HOPE

*The worker becomes an ever cheaper commodity
the more commodities he creates.*

—Karl Marx, *Economic and Philosophic
Manuscripts of 1844*

"The best thing you can do is to be positive, happy, and willing to do anything . . . without complaint."[1] So reads one of the countless pearls of wisdom for interns rattling around the Web. Other behavioral suggestions for interns include: smiling, saying "thank you," projecting humility, expressing enthusiasm for simple tasks. The overarching message is, exude cheerful gratitude at all times.[2] Whatever you think of your work or its educational value, act like you love it. Although the duties and compensation for the millions of interns around the globe can vary wildly from institution to institution, one quality that nearly all of them share is that they are a form of temporary work with little or no guarantee of continued employment.

The pay is not great, either, if it exists at all. Ross Perlin estimates that half of the 1 to 2 million interns in America today (a conservative estimate, by his venture) work without pay or for less than the federal minimum wage, when their work is broken down by hour.[3] There currently exist vast numbers of people working for little or no money, and these very people are exhorted to express gratitude and happiness while doing so. It's worth pausing to consider how very astonishing and yet how very common this situation is. Under capitalism, there is hardly a more perfect figure than the grateful unpaid worker.

What drives so many workers to compete for, and to gladly undertake, such exploitative labor? In a word: hope. In a 2013 study, media scholars Kathleen Kuehn and Thomas F. Corrigan penned the term *hope labor*, which Kuehn describes as "un- or undercompensated work, often performed in exchange for experience and exposure in hopes that future work will follow."[4] Hope is a powerful driver of cheap labor because it is internalized by the worker; it is what Lordon might call an "intrinsic affect." Other methods of extracting free or underrated labor typically entail external pressures, whether physical, as in prison labor or military conscription, or social, as in office peer pressure to work through lunch and respond to e-mail on weekends.[5] Hope, on the other hand, comes from within.

Initially, Kuehn and Corrigan devised the term *hope labor* to describe modes of uncompensated work they observed occurring online.[6] Independently, the authors noticed that users of the sports-blogging platform and social media site Sports Blog Nation (SB Nation) and the business review site Yelp happily generated free content for those sites as personal entertainment. However, many of the users also cited hope of future, compensated work as a secondary motivation, even if far-fetched. Perhaps a popular post on SB Nation would lead to paid sports punditry; attractive restaurant photos on Yelp might lead to contract work for a photographer.[7]

Much of this digital labor is directed specifically toward self-branding, Kuehn explained to me. For many "Yelpers," the utility of a review may be secondary to developing a unique, recognizable online identity associated with their user name. In fact, such free work in the online realm is frequently performed with the aim of projecting employability in the actual world. Thus much of this digital labor takes on an emotional, or affective, dimension. Workers put effort into offering not just samples of their work but also images of themselves as happy, eager, and affable.

The market doesn't just dangle well-paid, comfortable, apparently enjoyable work before the masses; it very carefully stokes and cultivates their hope. It does this in numerous industries by establishing tiered systems of work. Tiered, or two-track, labor forces abound across sectors from professional sports (minor- vs. major-league athletes) to academia (adjunct vs. tenured or tenure-track faculty) to office work and manufacturing (temporary vs. full-time employees). Workers in the top tiers frequently earn decent salaries, have stable, comfortable working conditions, and enjoy benefits such as premium employee-sponsored health care and paid leave. Bottom-tier workers are a more casual labor force, with contract or part-time schedules, drastically lower earnings, and fewer, if any, benefits or labor protections.

It is hope labor that undergirds the great array of tiered-work structures across the employment landscape. Medical residents, minor-league athletes, adjunct faculty, temp workers, and, of course, interns, in many cases, perform work close to or even identical to that of much better compensated colleagues in the same sectors. While part-time, casual work suits many workers, it's clear that the majority of these workers strive to enter the top tier and labor in the bottom tier with the expectation that they are at the beginning of a career pathway. Certain bottom-tier workers, including medical residents and trade apprentices, may reasonably expect to graduate into the top tier, and often there is a tangible separation of experience and skill level distinguishing them from top-tier workers, even if they occasionally perform the same tasks.

Often, however, relegation to the top or bottom tier is arbitrary. In many cases, bottom-tier workers often bear the same credentials and assume the same risks as their better-paid colleagues. Or, when differences in experience and credentials do exist, they don't necessarily justify the vast inequality of pay and labor conditions. Are star major-league baseball players, some of whom earn tens of millions of dollars or more, really 1,000 times more talented and enjoyable to watch than most minor-league players? Are adjunct faculty, many of whom bear PhD's from world-renowned programs and publish articles (and sometimes entire books) with the same top-flight publishers, really only a fraction as valuable as tenure-track faculty doing essentially the same tasks?

Employers have harnessed the full power of free-market competition to exploit human hope in creating labor structures that exploit increasing amounts of workers. A few plum jobs at the top for which increasing numbers of bottom-tier workers compete ever more desperately guarantees a cheap and disempowered workforce overall. They've figured out that people won't throw eighty-mile-per-hour pitches and teach Chaucer to college freshmen for $20,000 per year. They will, however, do it for $20,000 per year plus the hope of performing these tasks on better terms in the future. In fact, hope labor isn't merely normalized, it's institutionalized. The realization of "Henry," one of the interns Perlin writes about in his book *Intern Nation: How to Earn Nothing and Learn Little in the Brave New Economy*, is surely familiar to scores of job seekers: Henry noticed "every 'entry-level' job seemed to require two or three years of experience. 'How does that work? Where are you supposed to get it?'" he asked.[8]

Whether described as "paying one's dues" or "proving oneself," a significant time invested in undercompensated, bottom-tier hopeful work is now a prerequisite for full-time, salaried work in many sectors. Much of the labor force has so internalized this reality that those who bristle at the notion of bottom-tier purgatory and expect full-time jobs directly out of college or graduate programs are considered entitled. Hope is such a powerful ideological tool because, cultivated in specific ways, it facilitates identification with exploitative forces rather than the assertion of one's own interests.

OF INTERNS, ADJUNCTS, AND TEMPS

Although two-tiered labor systems abound and vary widely across sectors, I focus briefly here on interns, adjunct faculty, and temporary workers, because these are three of the fastest-growing pools of bottom-tier labor today within their various industries. Furthermore, these workers represent a sizable cross section of the skill and credential levels of those trying to make it in today's labor market. Adjunct faculty often—though not always—hold a master's degree or PhD, the highest degree a university can bestow. Other adjunct faculty nonetheless typically bear a high level of specialized knowledge, qualifying them to teach in higher education, across disciplines from accounting to dance. Temporary workers and interns, who work everywhere from factories to law firms, run the full gamut of educational backgrounds. The motivations, hopes, and needs for each worker are unique, but interns, adjuncts, and temps are united in that they often constitute cheap, disposable (or "flexible," in business speak) sources of labor.

Unlike most adjuncts and temporary workers who reluctantly accept these positions for lack of better options, many interns are frequently lured into low-paid or unpaid servitude by implied promises of valuable training, networking opportunities, and simple proximity to salaried workers in fields they hope to enter. Yet many end up disappointed, promptly forgotten by their employers upon the entry of the next season's intern crop. A 2014 *New York Times* article described an "intern glass ceiling" that prevents interns from breaking through into full-time, salaried work. "No one hires interns," sighed one recent college graduate who had held four internships but had yet to land a full-time job. Another confessed that she had sent out more than 300 job applications but only ever got acceptances for internship programs.[9] While many interns gain salaried employment post-internship, internships do not provide a clear or direct career pathway in the manner of an entry-level job.

Interns are caught in a vicious cycle. They work for cheap or free in hopes of becoming salaried, full-time employees in the field of their choice. But one of the pitfalls of interning is that once a worker has shown that he or she will work for free, employers have little incentive to pay him or her much afterward, especially with waves of eager, would-be interns washing up on their shores with every graduation season. Exacerbating this exploitative cycle is the dispiriting flaccidity of the post-2008 economic recovery. The majority of job growth in the United States is in low-wage sectors such as the service economy and care work, often insultingly dismissed as low skill. Furthermore, due to overmanagement and de-skilling, many once-attractive professional jobs like teaching have become less professional and hence less attractive. In other words, there simply isn't enough bliss-inducing work with comfortable pay and benefits to absorb all the college grads, laid-off workers, and career changers looking for work.

In fact, while the popular image of the intern may be a fresh-faced college grad, increasing numbers of older workers are willing to take internships, often after they've been laid off or have spent time outside the workforce, perhaps to care for children or other family members. Instead of turning these workers away, employers are more than happy to let them run errands and do light office work for extremely cheap wages. Fueled by hope, many workers cheerfully comply. A report for National Public Radio profiled two women who had worked recently as unpaid interns. Both had valuable experience: one was a former police officer and marina manager, the other held a master's degree in fine arts and had a former career in film and marketing. While the former police officer was still invested in her internship with the Red Cross, the other woman left hers and took paid work in a cafeteria, while she—at age fifty—casts about for a new career. "I just never expected to have to redesign my career, over and over and over again," she said.[10]

Hope also obscures many of the other concessions that interns, particularly unpaid interns, accede to. As Perlin notes, most interns do not question the legality of their working conditions. In most cases, it is in fact criminal not to pay workers according to the Fair Labor Standards Act (FLSA), which established a federal minimum wage, among other worker protections. People classified as trainees are not covered by the FLSA, but in order to be thus classified, a worker must meet six criteria as defined by the US Department of Labor. Among them are stipulations that there be actual educational value to the work performed, that the work benefits the trainee and is *not* for the benefit of the employer, and that trainees do not displace regular workers.[11] The conditions of most internships baldly fly in the face of these requirements. Many internships hold little educational value, benefit employers at the expense of interns, and are routinely established in order to avoid hiring paid workers.

Because interns are often classified as trainees, they essentially waive their rights to legal protections covering workers in instances of discrimination based on race, gender, or disability, injury on the job, or sexual harassment. Unfortunately, the interns who do discover just how flimsy their legal protections are, are typically those on the receiving end of the criminal activity described above.[12] It is at these moments that the perniciousness of work-for-hope rears its head and the dearth of tangible returns for work performed become painfully clear.

The gendered dimensions of hope-fueled intern labor are also significant. According to a report by the research and consulting firm Intern Bridge, in partnership with Phil Gardner at Michigan State University's Collegiate Employment Research

Institute, some 77 percent of unpaid interns are women.[13] Madeleine Schwartz, who has written about internships for *Dissent*, analyzes this glaring disparity from the perspective of free work, broadly speaking. Schwartz rightly encourages us to ask, "Who, traditionally, works for nonmonetary rewards?" The answer is women in the home: "Traditionally, women's work wasn't work. Cooking dinner or cleaning the floor, however long it took, unless it was done by a servant, wasn't labor— these were an expression of love and duty, an extension of a woman's natural role as a wife and mother. Why ask for monetary compensation, the belief went, when a satisfied family at the dinner table was the only fulfillment a woman needed?"[14] Although mainstream culture might reject the more reactionary assertions of this belief, particularly those about the "natural role" of women, in practice, such mores prove frustratingly intractable. Women still perform more than half of the child care and housework in heterosexual households in which both adults work full-time. And from their earliest days, girls are socialized to be accommodating and to avoid conflict. These deeply ingrained impulses carry over into the world of work outside the home. Regardless of a worker's gender, internships, insofar as they demand meekness, complicity, ceaseless demonstrations of gratefulness, and work for free or for very little pay put workers in a feminized position, which, historically, has been one of disadvantage.

Even when workers do eventually leave internships behind, the sacrifice in pay that they have made during these low-earning intern years can follow them for their entire working lives. The salary drawn during a worker's first job upon entering the labor force can affect subsequent earnings throughout his or her life. Those who earn more at the outset are able to cite their present salary in future wage negotiations, be they for raises or starting salaries at new jobs. In this way, workers build upon their employers' demonstrated testimony of their work's worth. Interns working for low pay or for free relinquish this crucial bargaining chip. Once a worker has shown he or she will work for very little, prospective employers are freer to downgrade wage offerings, as interns may be willing to take low-paying first jobs simply on account that a low wage is still better than what they earned as interns.

A report out of the Federal Reserve Bank in New York supports these conclusions. The Fed researchers found that the bulk of earnings growth in the United States occurs during workers' first decade in the workforce.[15] Since, for most workers, the "average earnings growth from ages 35 to 55 is zero" what they earn by age 35 is indicative of (though not explicitly determinative of) what they will earn over a lifetime of work, especially considering that most workers experience negative wage growth between ages 45 and 55.[16] What do these findings mean for young workers? Akane Otani of *Bloomberg News* puts it succinctly: "The time to hustle is when you're young. Because unless you're a fantastic anomaly, you'll probably see your last big raise well before your 40th birthday."[17] Wages gone unearned at the beginning of one's working life compound themselves later on. The opportunity cost of unearned income during an internship doesn't limit itself to the period of the internship but can follow workers for decades. Of course, because they remain in the realm of the hypothetical, unearned wages and compounded future unearned wages are easy for people to ignore in the face of a "glamorous" internship in an artist's studio or media company, especially if they've just entered the workforce and believe there's time to play catch-up. There isn't, and a lifetime of lost earnings is a heavy price to pay for hope.

The mushrooming of internship programs has coincided with the massive shift of teaching in higher education from tenured and tenure-track faculty to part-time instructors. The tenured or tenure-track professor is a salaried, full-time employee of a college or university. Most divide their time among teaching, conducting research, and other activities like advising. They have offices and are assisted by departmental secretaries. Upon a successful tenure review, a professor is often considered a lifetime employee of his or her school, barring extreme circumstances. When most people hear the word *professor*, what they picture—tweed elbow patches and all—is someone who is or has been on the tenure track. Faculty with part-time, or adjunct, appointments, by contrast, are contract instructors, typically paid per course. Because they don't have a permanent presence on campus, they often do not have access to offices or administrative support. They are not paid to conduct research. Often, they have no guaranteed employment at a school beyond the semester.

Like interns, adjuncts comprise a vastly diverse group, with multitudes of unique career goals and financial needs. For some, the part-time nature of the work is suitable. A choreographer, for instance, might teach a course at a local college in between productions. Or a retired lawyer with a distinguished career might guest-teach a course. These arrangements can work very well, fostering symbiotic relationships between school and community. They allow individuals outside of academia but with specialized knowledge to interact with students, and they allow schools to take full advantage of local resources off campus. And, indeed, many adjuncts today are served well by the part-time, contract nature of this work.

Things become problematic when large numbers of adjuncts are trying to support themselves and their families solely on adjunct wages, as is the situation presently. Working as an adjunct never paid very well, and it always paid far less than the salaries earned by those on the tenure track. In large part, this is because traditionally adjuncts are not expected to conduct research, advise dissertations, or participate in school governance like those on the tenure track. Colleges and universities do not invest in the long-term careers of adjuncts the way they do for tenure-track faculty. Like other low-wage work, most obviously fast-food work and a fair amount of retail work, adjunct jobs were initially considered side gigs, opportunities to earn a little extra to supplement another primary source of income.

Today, however, increasing numbers of adjuncts attempt to support themselves and their families solely by performing this work. Many scrape by, sometimes with the help of public-assistance programs, by cobbling together rosters of courses at multiple schools: $3,500 for a course at College A, $2,000 for another at University B. In terms of hours worked, many adjuncts are working full-time, well over forty hours per week, but earning in the neighborhood of $20,000 to $25,000 per year without benefits. Supporting a household on an income earned solely on adjunct wages is a daunting task. The Service Employees International Union (SEIU) calculated that in Boston, where the average per-course wage was between $3,750 and $5,225 at nonprofit institutions in 2013, an adjunct instructor might have to teach a nearly impossible twelve courses per year just to earn $45,000. The common course load for a tenure-track or tenured professor might be between two and five courses per year for an average salary of $83,000.[18] Of course, this higher salary also covers the substantial amount of research tenure-track faculty conduct, whereas adjuncts, if they wish to pursue independent research, must do it on their own time and dime.

This last reality is an especially problematic one for those adjuncts who are actively trying to get a tenure-track job. Adjunct work was never intended as an on-ramp to the tenure track in the vein of other off-tenure academic posts, such as postdoctoral fellowships. Most tenure-track job postings state that the hiring departments seek an "active research profile" in the ideal candidate. While many adjuncts admirably conduct substantive research on their own, unlike their colleagues on the tenure track, their research activity is uncompensated.

Only about a quarter of college and university instructors today are tenured or on the tenure track in the United States. Over several decades, many schools have shifted vast portions of teaching onto part-time adjuncts, even as the amount of teaching has increased—more Americans attend college now than ever before. There are myriad causes for this unfortunate situation, and they can fill entire books (indeed, they have). Suffice it to say that there are, simply, far more freshly minted PhD's than there are tenure-track jobs for them. So many bide their time, scratching out a meager living on adjunct appointments while continuing to apply for tenure-track jobs. However, as with interns, their work situation puts adjuncts in a bind, in that it can actually hinder career building. A congressional report on adjunct labor concluded that "problems with career advancement and professional support" are rife in contingent academic work: "Many contingent faculty take part-time work employment because it is the only job available in their desired field, hoping it will be a temporary detour on the way to full-time status. This detour, more often than not, becomes permanent."[19] The report continues:

> Adjuncts face systemic obstacles to career growth. Because they teach so many classes to piece together a living, they have little time to research and publish. Universities may pay for graduate students and tenured faculty to attend academic conferences, but adjuncts must usually travel to these events, where faculty recruiting often occurs, on their own dime. Despite these hurdles, respondents reported that on top of the hours they spend teaching, they published, attended conferences, and pursued professional development—*all with an eye to one day landing a coveted full-time job* [emphasis added].[20]

Why do adjuncts continue performing such high-skilled work for so little return? In hope of entering the top tier of the academic labor force.

Just as distressing as the shift of classroom teaching onto underpaid part-timers in academia is the shift of *research* onto cheap, temporary, off-tenure workers. This is increasingly the case in the biological sciences and medical research for which postdoctoral fellows, or postdocs, staff laboratories. Like adjunct faculty, postdocs in the sciences are highly skilled workers with advanced degrees working on short-term contracts. Postdocs are officially in training for tenure-track positions in the sciences, hoping to one day oversee the very kinds of labs in which they work. Yet only about 15 percent of postdocs in these fields will get a tenure-track job. As National Public Radio's Richard Harris puts it, they're "being trained for jobs that don't actually exist."[21] Yet this second-class, "shadow workforce" bolsters American science with labor performed in the hope of more stable employment.

Adjuncts and postdocs who strive to join the tenured ranks work in proximity to the jobs they desire—jobs that not only entail the actual work they wish to be doing, but also bestow salaried wages, health insurance and retirement benefits, regular schedules, long-term employment, and offices. Tantalizing closeness is the hallmark of second-class labor: it affords workers a clear view of what could be, yet they remain relegated to the frustration zone of so-close-yet-so-far. Second-class work is like sitting in the first row of economy class on an airplane; it affords an alluring glimpse of first class, but the mesh curtain separating the two proves a deceptively firm barrier.

Adjuncts don't garner much sympathy in the popular press, no doubt in part because holding a PhD is indeed a rare privilege. Why choose to keep performing undervalued work? These people have PhDs, they can do anything, so why do they stay? The answers to these questions are unique to each worker, and many adjuncts do indeed leave academia after several years or when they have decided continuing is financially untenable. On a practical level, many people who earn PhDs and plan for an academic career simply don't have the professional networks and experience required for other lines of work. If it takes someone six dedicated years to earn the degree, that's six years of not building up expertise and contacts in another sector. That, combined with an employment market that's weak across the board and throngs of interns willing to do entry-level work for free, makes career shifting especially difficult, and not just for academics.

In truth, however, hope and love are powerful forces for which people will sacrifice much. Just like tenured faculty, adjuncts are deeply passionate about their fields of study and care about their students. The hold that these motivations have on workers should not be underestimated or discounted. For centuries, Western culture has glorified romantic notions of the artist, the activist, the caregiver, the scholar, who works not for wages primarily, but instead for service to others, for renown, for "the greater good," and for the inherent rewards of the work itself. These values, like the gender conventions discussed briefly above, shape our sense of identity and the ways in which we perform our work. Although these various motivations are often noble in and of themselves, the less exalted reality is that work is overwhelmingly something individuals need to do in order to care for themselves and their families at the most basic levels. Holding fast to values like service to an academic discipline need not obscure or diminish this fact. Even when we become aware of the cultural determination of these values, and the ways in which they may not be serving us well, it is nonetheless extremely difficult to abandon them.

"It's for a week? Ten dollars an hour? You bet I'm comfortable with Excel!" These words, composed with sarcastic bite by writer Rob Bryan, encapsulate the outward gusto with which many workers accept temporary labor. Temporary, or temp, work pays about 25 percent less than permanent work in which employees perform similar or identical tasks, affords workers few workplace protections and, typically, no benefits, and is, as Bryan puts it, "too short to build a life on." During six years temping in offices, Bryan performed various short-term duties "from two-day gigs moving office furniture to six-month trudges through thousands of digitized invoices." In spite of his professed enthusiasm for spreadsheets, however, Bryan describes temp work as not just dispiriting but emotionally damaging on an existential level:

For me, the worst part about temp work wasn't the
boredom of being required to, say, sit in a mailroom all
day with no more than an hour of work to do, which
I mitigated by such measures as doing the crossword
puzzle or listening to *Purple Rain* in its entirety. Nor
was it the low pay, with which I had no higher-paying
work to compare. No, the worst part was the awareness
of my own disposability. . . .[22]

Bryan's descriptions of his work and his feelings about it
more or less align with the popular imagination of temp work
as the opposite of the fulfilling, lovable job. Perhaps rightly
so. Often, temp work is the definition of drudgery—grueling
physical labor, mind-dulling, repetitive office work. The pay
is significantly lower than that earned by permanent workers
in the same sectors, and benefits, not to mention simple ap-
preciation, are nearly nonexistent. In a DWYL world, why are
so many workers doing such tedious, low-paid, thankless, precarious work? The reverse question is equally pressing: why is
DWYL such a popular trope in the midst of such bleak employment conditions?

The answers to these questions lie in the systemic dis-
empowerment of workers. Workers are caught in an employment market that offers them few opportunities for which they
must nevertheless demonstrate enthusiastic submissiveness.

Temp-staffing agencies are booming: in 2012, the US Labor Department reported that the number of temporary workers had reached an all-time high of 2.7 million.[23] Temporary workers do everything from computer programming to assembly-line manufacturing, legal services to carpentry. Their educational backgrounds, skill sets, and career goals vary widely. What these workers have in common, both with one another and with adjuncts and interns, is that they remain a bottom-tier workforce in their various industries. In fact, it is this second class status of their working conditions—much more so than their temporary classification—that defines their experience as workers. Repeated studies show that most temps wish to be permanent workers.[24] Yet employers have become addicted to expendable labor that is cheap at least in the short term.

As Erin Hatton writes in *The Temp Economy: From Kelly Girls to Permatemps in Postwar America*, the temp industry grew itself by casting workers to employers not as resources but as burdensome costs that ought to be reduced as much as possible.[25] According to what Hatton calls the "liability model" of management, labor costs and profits are in a zero-sum opposition to each other. The more an employer can reduce worker costs through wage cuts, de-skilling, speed-ups, and layoffs, the greater his profits, or so the theory goes. Unsurprisingly, this rational liability model has its roots in the earliest days of management theory, which saw the rise of an independent managerial class antagonistic to labor, as discussed in the previous chapter.

In order to recruit workers, agencies presented temping as an opportunity for excitement and self-fulfillment. Yet again we return to the uncompensated housewife: "The next time you get fed up with the household routine, join the Kelly Girl Service," beckons a man in a 1961 recruitment film for the temp agency.[26] According to Hatton, projecting temp work as feminine, white, and middle-class served a number of ends. To the agency's clients, these demographic characteristics signaled that temp workers weren't looking for family-supporting salaries or benefits like paid sick leave, nor were temps comprised of more "threatening" outsiders like blacks and recent immigrants looking to infiltrate the office. Finally, the image of the obliging Kelly Girl helping in the office to earn some extra "pin money" was meant to avoid antagonizing labor unions concerned with protecting traditionally male industrial work.[27]

The Kelly Girl—that well-off, genteel woman working for pin money—was always a ruse, and indeed today's popular image of the office temp is more akin to what Bryan describes. The truth that often goes unmentioned, however, is that "today, many temps work for years in the same place, their status not so much temporary but defined by a triangular work arrangement in which a temp agency is a worker's legal employer who contracts his work out to its business clients."[28] In other words, temps are not really temporary at all, but simply a more precarious and enfeebled workforce.

Temps are, however, often placed side by side with permanent workers, and this proximity stokes hope. As labor journalist Sarah Jaffe reports, many temps, particularly in manufacturing, wish to become "employees," but the path to achieving permanent status is unclear. One auto-manufacturing temp Jaffe interviewed thought he had achieved permanent status upon a promotion, only to find that his new position had been reclassified as temporary. These so-called permatemps work for the same employers for years, even earning promotions, but never shedding their temp status. "It's not a 'temp' job," one worker remarks, "but it's temp status."[29] In other words, employers are using the temp classification as a cover to pay lower wages, cut health-care costs, and skirt labor protections to which permanent workers are legally entitled.

Many workers find themselves trapped. "Despite the many drawbacks of a temp job, anemic job growth during the economic recovery has meant that many blue-collar workers have few options beyond putting in their time as a temp in the hope that they'll get hired full-time one day," Jaffe writes, continuing, "The lure of that elusive job is used to keep permatemps around."[30] Jaffe's reporting demonstrates the dark side of hope—its punitive potential. By stringing temps along with hope, employers gain a workforce that is cowed, disposable, and cheap.

Temp work need not mean endlessly toiling in hope. In fact, permatemping is effectively illegal in several countries. As part of a ProPublica investigation of temp work, Michael Grabell and Lena Groeger report that many countries implement time limits on temp work, after which companies are required to hire temps full-time. Other countries require equal pay for equal work and bar temps from performing hazardous work better handled by experienced or thoroughly trained workers.[31]

These measures should provide encouragement—actual, positive, energizing hope, as opposed to timorous longing—to aspirational workers everywhere. Many workers, even top-tier workers with salaries and benefits, perform their labor with an eye toward promotion or other jobs—doing so need not be exploitative. For contingent, or bottom-tier, workers, however, hope labor often requires the abandonment of hope for the improvement of present working conditions because these conditions are imagined to be temporary, which, often, they are not.

Some interns and contingent workers are beginning to reject this premise. Increasingly, fed-up interns are taking their employers to court, suing for back wages, and many are winning. In a landmark case, two production interns who worked on the set of the film *Black Swan* sued Fox Searchlight, claiming that the company had violated minimum-wage laws. The interns had performed tasks usually undertaken by paid employees for free, such as taking lunch orders, answering phones, and making travel arrangements for other employees. In his ruling in favor of the interns, New York State Federal District Judge William H. Pauley III stated, "Undoubtedly [the interns] received some benefit from their internships, such as résumé listings, job references, and an understanding of how a production office works." He continued, "But those benefits were *incidental* to working in the office *like any other employees* and were not the result of internships intentionally structured to benefit them" [emphasis added].[32] Scores of lawsuits filed by former interns have followed in the wake of Judge Pauley's ruling.[33]

Interns have also launched public awareness campaigns. During London Fashion Week in February 2013, the advocacy group Intern Aware handed out tote bags bearing the phrase PAY YOUR INTERNS. Meant to resemble the gift bags given to guests at runway shows, the bags contained information about British minimum-wage laws and the group itself.[34]

Adjunct instructors, too, have started to make demands of their employers. Although many adjuncts understand that they may never even have the opportunity to gain tenure, they can still advocate for nonpoverty wages, longer-term contracts, institutional support to conduct their own research, paid family leave, and health and retirement benefits. Through the campaign Adjunct Action, the Service Employees International Union (SEIU) has begun organizing adjuncts in cities across the United States.

Unions have also turned an eye toward organizing temps, particularly in blue-collar and service industries, though this proves a daunting task given that the temps' official employers are not the companies where they work but a myriad of staffing agencies (in fact, some companies may draw temps from several agencies simultaneously). American temps are beginning to score some legislative victories as well. In August 2014, the California state legislature passed Assembly Bill 1897, which would hold temp-staffing agencies liable for cheating workers out of their wages (many temps pay fees to their agency, which sometimes puts their take-home pay below the minimum wage) or recklessly exposing them to harm (ProPublica revealed that temps are far more likely to suffer severe, even deadly injuries on the job than permanent workers are).[35]

HOPE AND CLASS

The burgeoning labor movements described briefly above represent a significant departure from somnambulant dedication to hope labor. Workers from university seminar rooms to assembly lines are insisting that worker protections meet their needs far better than hope does. For many of these workers, particularly those in white-collar environments and bearing advanced degrees, their actions are forcing them to confront their status as laborers for the first time.

The paradox of DWYL is that, while exhorting people to perform work that they love, it denies that this work is work at all. Persuading professional workers not to think of themselves as workers is one of the profoundest achievements of established class rhetoric. When people speak of the working class as a constituency to which they do not belong, embedded in their speech is a disavowal of their own status as workers, specifically as workers toiling for an employer or entity other than themselves. The social desire not to fall into this class is so powerful that, as we've seen, people will assume massive amounts of debt, submit to intrusive surveillance and managerial control, and work for hope instead of wages. This, too, is a disavowal of their own work.

Hope remains a major force keeping the swelling reserve army of credentialed, would-be professionals toiling for paltry wages (or no wages at all). While scores of college grads working for free in unpaid internships could be doing paid apprenticeships that impart tangible skills, they opt for the uncompensated purgatory of coffee fetching and photocopying in the hope that such service will lead to a lucrative, lovable job. Is it worth it?

Being a unionized sheet-metal worker may pay the bills, and it may even be enjoyable in that it bestows a sense of accomplishment at the end of a shift or pride in a craft well executed. Such work may instill a sense of pleasure in that it facilitates the care and well-being of the worker's family and loved ones. Yet these are not the fashionable joys of work, dismissed as naive and insufficiently ambitious, particularly after the greed-is-good 1980s. Apparently, for a fair portion of the population, the only joys of work that count are the ones that facilitate a complete, narcissistic identification with the job and bestow the accoutrements of upper-middle-class existence. Superficially, sheet-metal work isn't a job that pretends to bestow "intrinsic joyful affects" to the liberal-arts-degree-holding throngs. But a statement on the Sheet Metal Workers International Association (SMWIA) Web site is remarkable: "The SMWIA strives to establish and maintain desirable working conditions for its members through their employers. Doing so provides them that measure of comfort, happiness, and security to which every member is entitled in return for his or her highly trained and skilled labor."[36] Comfort, happiness, and security in return for skilled labor—is this not the collective wish of commencement-address audiences at $60,000-per-year schools?

Class anxiety not only fuels DWYL culture, but this anxiety also exacerbates already widening class divisions. Despite earning very little or nothing at all, interns still manage to survive. Who is subsidizing this work then? Parents who can afford it, the occasional high-earning partner, the very occasional inheritance.[37] Which academics are able to hold out the longest in low-paid adjunct appointments while searching for tenure-track jobs? Those with independent resources. While tiered work systems may appear at first to be meritocratic, fostering competition to sift the best workers out for the top tiers, such structures typically favor the wealthy and well connected.

Tiered work systems also exert downward pressure on workers, pushing many into (or deeper into) poverty. With few benefits or labor protections, temporary workers, the bottom-tier workers in manufacturing and the service industry, pay a higher price than do permanent workers when visited by the vicissitudes of life. For them, a day at home recovering from illness costs a day's wages because many lack paid sick leave; a workplace injury can quickly lead to a lifetime of devastating health-care debt, as they aren't afforded health insurance and aren't granted workers' compensation.

The meritocracy justification for tiered work systems is too often a red herring. As we've seen, often these tiers are arbitrary or set in place to exploit desperation in a weak employment market, extracting below-rate labor from workers with few other options. Rather than facilitating merit-determined paths to stable careers, ever more workers are pushed down into their respective bottom tiers—interns, adjunct faculty, and temporary workers have all increased greatly in number as opportunities for professional entry-level work, tenure-track positions, and permanent work have declined or stalled. At the same time, these workers must not only perform the tasks of their work, but also the emotional work of demonstrating how very eager they are to do this work, in hopes that their goodwill might catch the eye of a top-tier gatekeeper.

Perhaps one of the most dispiriting things about tiered work systems is that they fragment workforces and encourage divisiveness. They are simultaneously self-perpetuating and self-validating. Those who do graduate to the top tier sometimes view the relegation of their peers to bottom-tier work as legitimate, evidence that the system is just. Because the system worked for them, it works, period, and because these graduates are in relative positions of power, they often consciously or unconsciously continue the bifurcated organization of labor in their sectors. But overcoming this divisiveness is important. Marc Bousquet writes, "In theory there is no such thing as 'an adjunct.' There are only faculty members with adjunct appointments."[38]

Of course, some interns, adjuncts, and temps do "make it." If breaking through to the top tier were truly impossible, there would be nothing to fuel the hope of the bottom tier. When Kuehn spoke with me about how she and Corrigan settled on the term *hope labor* for describing undercompensated, aspirational work, as opposed to using other descriptors like *fantasy*, she stated that temporality of hope was critical to them. Hope es an achievable reality, one in the foreseeable future.

It is precisely this just-around-the-corner, any-day-now temporality that is so beguiling and encourages such dedication on the part of workers. What hope labor ultimately manifests is a belief in the employment marketplace's justness, faith that it correctly sorts workers into appropriate terms of labor. By following the rules of capitalist competition more ardently and with more demonstrable affirmation of their rectitude, the thinking goes, a worker will attain the type of employment he or she desires on comfortable terms. Thus the opposite of hope labor is revolutionary action or the total disbelief in the methods by which work is distributed. But the temporality of hope encourages the most vulnerable workers to double down on the very system that exploits them. There's little impetus to abandon hope of a good life when it appears just within grasp.

4

NO REST

*He whose feet rest, and whose hands no longer toil,
may keep the golden wheels of the mind working
all the more.*

—Henry Ward Beecher, "Moral Theory of Civil
Liberty," sermon (1869)

*Far from idleness being the root of all evil,
it is rather the only true good.*

—Søren Kierkegaard, *Either/Or* (1843)

A favorite coffee shop from my college days sold T-shirts printed with the phrase SLEEP IS FOR THE WEAK. In line with this philosophy, the coffee there was extremely strong, served by a boisterous, always hustling crew behind the counter. On the spectrum of coffeehouses, it is the buzzy antithesis of old-world Viennese cafés with newspapers hanging on wooden racks, where one sits for an hour or more, served by a quietly decorous waitstaff. There are coffee shops that provide a rush, and ones that provide a retreat from it.

There's a reason why the Viennese café conjures nostalgia for a past world of Fraktur print and ivory-handled canes. The triumph of the rush model over the retreat model of the coffeehouse in terms of franchise proliferation is driven by forces both cultural and economic, although these forces are, of course, tightly intertwined. Most basically, it is easier to turn a profit by selling large volumes of eyelid-opening coffee in paper cups to queues of people on their way to work than it is by serving *Wiener Mélange* on a silver tray to patrons ensconced at marble-topped tables, leisurely reading the newspaper. More broadly, however, sleep has gone the way of the two-hour weekday lunch, demoted in public esteem to something primarily for the lazy, the decadent, the "weak."

Thanks to modern communication and the Internet, we are always afforded the opportunity to participate in the marketplace, an opportunity that capitalism relentlessly urges us to take. With even nonworking hours taken over by market activity—during most of our leisure time, we are consuming something: media, entertainment, transportation—sleep has become the most striking, often the only refuge from the cycle of consumption and production in daily life. No wonder capitalism has launched a multifront attack on sleep,[1] with consumable products (energy drinks, late-night television) and antisleep agitprop ("sleep is for the weak," valorization of unsleeping CEOs).

DWYL rhetoric is a critical tool in the cultural campaign to promote overwork and sleep deprivation by packaging these as self-fulfilling. After all, ideal love is nothing if not constant. The ceaselessly productive worker, with little time for rest, let alone any need or desire for it, stands as a heroic icon, particularly in the high-strung white-collar milieus of Silicon Valley and Wall Street. In this context, DWYL doesn't present the precious, feminized image of the self-employed designer dwelling in her chic studio while raking it in on Etsy. Rather, it takes on a hypermasculine cast. The desired persona is one that transcends needs for sleep, care, relationships, and any other obligation that might distract from work and profit. In this world, legendary figures are the ones who remain in the office for one hundred hours straight, working through their children's musical recitals and 104-degree fevers.[2] The idea is that workers become superhuman through the refusal of self-care.

Notably, the women who thrive in this environment tend not to be path breakers so much as über-conformists. As Sarah Leonard notes in her article on Yahoo! CEO Marissa Mayer, the latter topped *Business Insider*'s list of "19 Successful People Who Barely Sleep." Leonard writes of Mayer's famous refusal to take maternity leave:

> Rather than a reflection of Mayer, this is an impressive absorption of female biology into a reinforcement of the work ethic. Everyone knows that men can work all the time by ignoring their families. But women give birth. They're natural nurturers. What if they can perform *both roles* and somehow center motherhood *and* CEOship? She becomes a superworker, "balancing" two loads too heavy to be borne in any proportion.

Leonard continues, "Women's desire to break the glass ceiling right under [notorious workaholic Steve] Jobs's feet reinforces the importance of a brutal, dehumanizing schedule. Women can do that too. Only more."[3] And indeed Mayer is a master of "only more"; at Google, she was known for her 130-hour workweeks. It's impossible to be "more" of a worker than that. Women can succeed in the workaholic, hierarchical world of tech—for all its talk of disruption, it retains the long hours and exclusions of other private sectors—not by questioning the fairness or fundamental merit of its ground rules, but by following them more intensely.

But "only more" isn't merely depressing; it's outright dangerous. In 2013, a twenty-one-year-old intern at Bank of America Merrill Lynch's London office died suddenly. He had been working until 6 a.m. for three consecutive days. In the summer of 2014, a long-haul truck driver overturned his vehicle on the New Jersey Turnpike, severely injuring comedian Tracey Morgan and killing a companion of Morgan's. The truck driver had not slept in more than twenty-four hours.[4] Less headline grabbing are the more mundane degradations that overwork and sleep deprivation visit on the body: increased rates of illness, anxiety, depression, even coronary heart disease.[5]

All of these instances—from sudden, untimely deaths to worn-out immune systems unable to fend off another cold—are the consequences of the extent to which we've allowed work to dominate our lives. Outside the pantheon of high-earning super-workers, everyone is getting less sleep and working longer hours. In industries from medicine to long-haul trucking, grinding schedules that colonize ever more of our waking (and sleeping) hours are a point of pride. This is the case despite the fact that studies continually show that overwork is counterproductive.

The futility of overwork was accepted wisdom in manufacturing for decades. Hundreds of studies from the 1930s through the 1960s confirmed that employers were no better off working employees for ten-hour days instead of eight-hour days or for six-day weeks instead of five-day weeks. Paying workers to stick around an extra day merely evaporated profits. Furthermore, catastrophic accidents that "disable workers, damage capital equipment, shut down the lines, open the company to lawsuits, and upset shareholders" are greatly reduced when a workforce is well rested.[6]

The one exception to this common sense, what Sara Robinson calls "the overtime exception," is that it is possible to boost worker productivity by pushing workers to sixty- and seventy-hour workweeks for short periods. However, today, the critical "for short periods" qualification is largely forgotten. It's been long known that at these hours, productivity starts falling off after a couple of weeks. Grueling schedules can even produce negative value, for instance, when software teams lose ground over a series of weeks because they're so exhausted that they make more errors than they can fix in a given time frame.[7] Not only does productivity decline when employees are overworked, but after a "crunch period" of sixty-plus-hour weeks, it takes several *more* weeks after they have resumed their normal forty-hour weeks for productivity to reach its pre-crunch level. Consequently, effective managers understand that it's best to avoid overtime bursts altogether.[8]

There are numerous reasons for the disappearance of the forty-hour workweek, but Robinson singles out work cultures that promote worker passion as one of them. She sees this culture taking root first in the defense and then in the tech industries in late twentieth-century California. During the Cold War, defense companies like Lockheed in the Santa Clara Valley drew scores of ambitious scientists; these workers seemed to share certain personality traits, including social awkwardness, emotional detachment, and, namely, a single-mindedness about their work to the point at which "they devoted every waking hour to it, usually to the exclusion of nonwork relationships, exercise, sleep, food, and even personal care." In the late '50s, Lockheed's own company psychologists created a label for this particular bundle of traits: "the sci-tech personality."[9]

Managers had found a type of worker who gladly put aside, seemingly for the long term, nonwork desires and obligations, and even the most basic physical needs of hygiene and sleep. These workers were branded not as worrisome but as "passionate," with all the positive connotations of that word. And by the 1980s, a valley full of "passionate" workers was fertile ground for a burgeoning tech industry. Passionate overworkers like Steve Jobs became icons, not just to tech workers but also to the culture at large.

With passion as a new workplace requirement, it needed to be measured in some way, so that the passion of individual workers could be compared and used to mete out rewards and punishments. Enter the managers, who resorted to the laziest, most easily graphable, least imaginative way possible to gauge this intangible quality: hours spent in the office.[10] This intractable policy remains largely in place today. "We just don't know any other way to measure [workers], except by their hours," an office manager sighed to a team of workplace consultants in 2014.[11] This exasperation was aired a year after the consultants did a study of the same workplace, which revealed that employees were more productive when encouraged to take intermittent breaks and were (gasp) "permitted to leave as soon as they had accomplished a designated amount of work."[12]

Passion as measured by hours has put the workweek on a course of runaway inflation, to the point at which people are actually shortening their lives and endangering others—sometimes in sudden, tragic form—in pursuit of an ever-elusive ideal of capitalistic individualism.

Why do we allow ourselves to continue like this? If, according to DWYL, the pleasure of work derives from the very act of production, what are workers doing during all of those surplus hours when they are not, well, producing or producing only poorly? Why are salaried workers lingering in the office after their work is done or when they're beyond the point of meaningful production, only making themselves less effective in the long term?

The answer clearly has nothing to do with economic rationality and everything to do with ideology. Although

simple Excel charts may present the flimsiest guise of empiri-
cal, objective data about workers' supposed passion, the truth is
that passion doesn't equal hours spent in the office, nor does it
necessitate burning oneself out. Passion is all too often a cover
for overwork cloaked in the rhetoric of self-fulfillment. The
falsity of passion-as-hours logic is that, quite simply, it produces shoddy work, which is not what someone who is ostensibly passionate about his or her work would allow. Emphasizing
passion as a value in employees diminishes other potential—
seemingly obvious—attitudes toward work that have more to
bear on the quality of the work itself, things like competence
and good faith.

Passion, overwork, and 24/7 temporality are linked together by much more than the need for simple managerial
metrics. Cederström and Fleming argue that work today is of
such a nature that it exploits workers not only during their time
in the workplace, but also in their very act of living. Employers
seek to capture our "human qualities like social intelligence,
reciprocity, communication, and shared initiative." They add,
"The traditional point of production—say the factory assembly line—is scattered to every corner of our lives since it is now
our very sociality that creates value for business."[13] This logic
applies to nearly every level of the workforce, from the public
face an executive provides for his corporation to barista small
talk. When personal authenticity is demanded every moment

at work, "our authenticity is no longer a retreat from the mandatory fakeness of the office, but the very medium through which work squeezes the life out of us."[14] If everyone is always working anyway and the distinctions between our work and nonwork selves are muddled, staying in the office for an extra hour or three doesn't seem a terribly significant decision. And when a worker has internalized a DWYL ethic, it hardly seems like a decision at all.

Crucial to maintaining the culture of overwork and 24/7 temporality is the pervasive insecurity embedded in the belief that we are in unceasing competition with every other member of humanity. This feeling of unease is omnipresent, structuring our emotions and relationships outside of the workplace. Gilles Deleuze writes that "the corporation is a spirit, a gas,"[15] meaning that people no longer experience coercive control as masses within the walls of physical enclosures (schools, factories, prisons), but that today we are controlled outside of and in between these enclosures, through the competitive logic of the corporation. In a postindustrial world, this gaseous form of control becomes ever more necessary as production becomes increasingly untethered to physical locations of containment and workforces become more diffuse and workers more flexible.

This anxiety-driven form of control is not only pervasive and unceasing but atomizing as well. Each member of society is an individual capitalist, endlessly competing against everyone else. Deleuze briefly mentions "merit pay" for schoolteachers to exemplify his point; under this pay scheme, teachers are no longer a bloc of workers, but each fully divided from his or her peers.[16] It's no coincidence that the rise of such logic coincides with the dwindling power of labor unions overall. As institutions of solidarity that work to establish strict temporal and spatial zones of work and nonwork, unions are in every way anathema to the atomizing, pervasive control logic Deleuze describes. Solidarity becomes suspect when each individual views his- or herself as an independent contractor, locked in a zero-sum battle with the rest of society. Every moment he or she spends not working means someone else is getting ahead, to his or her detriment. Overwork, then, isn't an expression of passion but the manifestation of anxiety and alienation. DWYL rhetoric repackages this anxiety and alienation as ameliorating, good feelings or, in Kathi Weeks's characterization of Weber's work ethic, works to "deliver workers to their own exploitation."[17]

While Deleuze articulates the pervasiveness of corporate control outside the disciplinary enclosures such as the school and the prison, it is also important to remember that this form of control hasn't displaced the discipline of enclosure, only joined it. As Crary writes, "*Contra* Deleuze, the use of harsh physical confinement is greater today than at any time previously, in an expanding network of deliriously panoptic prisons.

His evocation of open, amorphic spaces without boundaries is belied by the brutal deployment of walled borders and closed frontiers, both of which strategically target specific populations and regions."[18] Within the workplace, discipline has only grown more intense, with both swelling management apparatuses and more penetrative surveillance techniques, as discussed in chapter 2. At the same time that coercive control diffuses into the overall environment, urging us to constantly produce (and consume the products pushed on us), disciplinary techniques within the work space tighten their grip.

This situation thoroughly benefits those in the capital-holding class who seek to extract the maximum possible labor from the most thoroughly cowed workforce. With enclosures (specifically workplaces) under increasingly greater discipline and the spaces between enclosures dominated by the controlling logic of the corporation, there is no physical refuge, nor any moment of the day without pressure to participate in the marketplace.

It was not supposed to be this way. Technological development paired with robust workers' movements indicated, for a time, that we would all be working fewer hours, not more. Historian Benjamin Kline Hunnicutt opens his book *Free Time: The Forgotten American Dream* with a startling observation: from the beginning of the nineteenth century, working hours in the United States were drastically reduced, cut in half by many estimates, over the course of a hundred years. The same was true of other industrialized nations.[19] Many thinkers, from John Maynard Keynes to Frank Lloyd Wright, anticipated technology's liberating potential.[20] Keynes predicted that across the board standards of living would increase as working hours decreased (specifically to fifteen-hour workweeks), and that humanity's material needs would be so thoroughly satisfied that we would "devote our energies to *non-economic purposes*" [emphasis added].[21] He even cautioned that we would have to get creative in devising ways to spend all of our free time. Keynes sanguinely titled the essay in which he penned these words "Economic Possibilities for Our Grandchildren." In it, he also predicted an end to the worst manifestations of the Protestant work ethic:

> When the accumulation of wealth is no longer of high social importance, there will be a great change to the code of morals. We shall be able to rid ourselves of many of the pseudo-moral principles which have hag-ridden us for two hundred years, by which we have exalted some of the most distasteful of human qualities into the position of the highest virtues.[22]

To many, the reduction in working hours that had occurred during the previous century was indicative of human progress and liberation. With increasing goods and services generated with reduced man hours thanks to the wonders of technology, people would finally be free from burdensome work and, hence, able to realize their full humanity, "delighting in nature, the body, and comradeship and struggling with life's tragedies and the challenges of the spirit and of the day."[23]

The cultural pendulum began to swing in the other direction, back in favor of increased working hours, after the Great Depression and the Second World War. Beginning at this time, a complete reversal in the common attitude toward work and leisure occurred: essentially, societal progress was redefined from liberation from work to economic growth. In order to pull the nation out of economic depression, President Franklin Roosevelt adopted and promoted a policy of full-time, full employment (at forty hours per week). Labor unions initially resisted this initiative, sticking to their traditional advocacy of shorter hours and higher wages. As they had been before the war, union leaders remained skeptical that economic growth on its own would sustain Roosevelt's Full-Time, Full Employment policy. Labor continued to maintain that shorter working hours were "part of a general national progress."[24]

Later on during the postwar years, however, the biggest labor organizations gradually abandoned their shorter-hours platforms and embraced full-time (forty hours per week) employment as the path to progress and prosperity for their members. Hunnicutt writes, "What labor had always seen as the conjoined-twin constituents of progress—shorter hours and higher wages—had divided, the one emerging as labor's cardinal objective, and the other relegated to a subordinate role."[25]

Explanations for labor's about-face on shorter hours abound. Given that it occurred during the Cold War, historians have proposed possibilities ranging from the expulsion of communists and radicals from labor organizations to new cultures of consumerism. However, none of these individual events entailed the adoption of a completely adverse ideology as did the union leaders' embrace of the growth model.[26] In fact, anticommunism and consumerism were folded into this ideology. Instead of allowing technological developments to pick up as much of the labor burden as possible, then distributing what remained to be done among workers, thus drastically reducing everyone's hours, this new approach promoted "national economic planning to create full employment and sustained economic growth."[27]

There had always been resistance to the shorter-hours movement on the part of capitalists and many (but by no means all) employers. For one hundred years, they fought a losing battle. However, once labor decided to put its faith in economic growth at the expense of its shorter-hours platform, once there was no one to resist pressure from owners and managers for more working hours, the floodgates opened. The results have been devastating: those fortunate enough to be employed are putting in more hours than ever (often at multiple jobs), and at the same time, it has become all too clear during the post-2008 recovery that economic growth on its own does little to alleviate unemployment and poverty. It the worst of all possible worlds: those with employment toil harder and longer for diminishing returns, while millions can find no work at all.

Today, the opposite of Keynes's optimistic vision has come to pass: we live in a world in which previously noneconomic purposes—including simple preferences in the form of our likes and favorites—are captured for corporate profit. The noneconomic has been made economic.

It's tempting to wonder whether capitalism hadn't doomed us to this fate from the very beginning. In *24/7*, Crary draws upon Marx's *Grundrisse* to foreground the relentless colonization of our time and even our personal thoughts, dreams, and preferences by the marketplace. In 1858, Marx wrote that capital exists in a state of "*constant continuity*." Value metamorphoses unceasingly: from money to commodity to exchange value to use value.[28] "In effect," Crary notes, "Marx is positing 24/7 temporalities as fundamental to the workings of capital; he understood that these durational processes [of capitalism, such as production and transport] were also metamorphic."[29] In considering the constant continuity of capital, the irrationality behind counterproductive overwork comes into clearer focus. If capitalism is more about process (constant continuity) than products or actually servicing people's needs, then naturally the impetus will be to keep workers working, regardless of whether they do it poorly or not.

The constant continuity of capital is a point reiterated by Siegfried Kracauer in his famous essay "The Mass Ornament." Kracauer saw the tightly coordinated, repetitive movements of Rockette-style dance troupes such as the Tiller Girls, popular in the 1920s and '30s, as reflective of capitalist production. In order to create kaleidoscopic formations, each dancer ceded her individuality to become part of a collectively moving mass. The patterns formed by the bodies were pointedly pointless, ornamental only, with no deeper meaning. "Like the mass ornament," Kracauer writes, "the capitalist production process is an end in itself. The commodities that it spews forth are not actually produced to be possessed; rather they are made for the sake of a profit that knows no limit."[30] The only logic that this system appreciates is the dumb logic of more: more legs in the kick line, more widgets coming out of the factory, another hour at the office. It will not brook any interruption, whether spurred by needs emotional (time caring for loved ones) or biological (sleep). Kracauer writes, "Since the principle of the *capitalist production process* does not arise purely out of nature, it must destroy the natural organisms that it regards either as means or as resistance. Community and personality perish when what is demanded is calculability. . . ."[31]

Attending the theatrical performance of one's child faces long odds against the obligations of capitalist production.

The decision to adhere to unproductive overwork is guided strongly by the work ethic, to return to Weber. Yet as Weeks has shown in her analysis of Weber's text, the work ethic is rife with destabilizing antinomies that threaten to undermine it. For instance, she points out that according to its original Protestant premise, the work ethic casts human toil as a means to quell anxieties about being among the elect. However, since salvation was predetermined, work could not be the means to it, only outward signs of it, at most. Weeks writes, "To the extent that work acquires more meaning as an act of signification than as production, there is something ritualistic about our adherence to its discipline,"[32] echoing Kracauer's point about the nonproductiveness of capitalism. Generative of neither material production nor spiritual reward, the entire premise of the work ethic begins to unravel and fall in on itself.[33]

After more than half a century of increasing work hours, pockets of resistance have begun to emerge. (And indeed, once we've arrived at the 130-hour workweek, there simply isn't any more time left to devote to capitalist production.) Unsurprisingly, many of these pockets are in Western Europe, where labor unions and political parties have not ceded nearly as much ground as their American counterparts during the postwar years of economic liberalization (though they still ceded plenty).

In France, labor groups have moved vigorously to protect their hard-won thirty-five-hour workweek against the work creep facilitated by smartphones and other means of electronic communication. In 2014, employers' federations and labor unions representing some 250,000 workers in technology and consultancy sectors agreed to a measure stipulating that employees are not accountable for answering work e-mail after 6 p.m., nor are they to experience any pressure to do so.[34] Workers in Daimler's German offices now have the option of installing a program, Mail on Holiday, that automatically deletes any e-mail entering an employee's work account while he or she is on vacation. (The sender receives a notice that his or her e-mail has been deleted, accompanied by the employee's return date and an alternate contact.)[35] These measures speak to the lines that workers are determined to hold in order to protect their nonworking time.

Elsewhere, activists have gone further, working to actually shorten working hours rather than merely ensuring that they don't expand. The city of Gothenburg received lots of wistful coverage in the American and UK press for experimenting with a six-hour workday for municipal employees. The city is evaluating the health and productivity of workers during a trial period against a control group working traditional eight-hour days. While Gothenburg remains committed to a capitalist schema of productivity as opposed to simply doing less work, the experiment does reflect skepticism toward the false logic of overwork.

In Britain, one of the country's prominent physicians, Dr. John Ashton, president of the UK Faculty of Public Health, recently called for the country to establish a four-day workweek, citing concerns about the adverse health effects of overwork, such as high blood pressure, sleep problems, and increased rates of infection due to stress. Taking a page from the labor movement's old playbook, Dr. Ashton also advocated for the four-day workweek as a means to reduce unemployment. He emphasized that "maldistribution of work," in which large numbers of workers are overworked while many remain unemployed, inflicts stress-related health problems upon both groups.[36]

Even in the workaholic United States, workers have begun to at least consider the benefits of reduced working hours. Recently, Al Jazeera America profiled a Portland tech start-up with a four-day workweek. The founders affirmed that their workers took few sick days and were highly productive.[37] In the wake of the banking intern's tragic death mentioned previously, several major investment banks have begun requiring that their young analysts, for whom 100-hour workweeks are routine, take one day off per week to rest. Even Marissa Mayer, she of the legendary 130-hour workweek, has extended parental leave at Yahoo! since taking the helm.

One detail stands out in these anecdotes: most of these changes and suggestions have come from the top down, from human resources departments, founders, CEOs, managers, and prominent public figures. In fact, one of the founders of the Portland start-up remarked, "I think [such policy] has to come from the CEOs or executives or founders."[38] We know from history that this hasn't always been true, and it's important to caution that radical changes in reducing working hours aren't going to come unless workers themselves start realizing their power and making bolder demands. Dr. Ashton's suggestions are inspiring, but inspiration remains just that unless workers take action.

Another important commonality in the above examples is class: workers at the tech start-up, Yahoo!, Daimler, the city of Gothenburg, and Wall Street banks are largely college-educated, professional workers enjoying benefits like employee-sponsored retirement plans and health care. It is certainly true that professional workers, particularly in the American tech and finance industries, put in long hours. The hours are part of the culture of these sectors, a point of pride as much as an acknowledged detriment to health and human relationships. But as much as professional workers humblebrag or talk about working eighty hours per week or more, heroically ignoring their bodies' cries for sleep, taken as a whole, one class of workers sleeps even less than they do: the working poor.

Olga Khazan reports that in the United States, about half of the people in households netting $30,000 per year or less sleep six or fewer hours per night, while only about a third of those in households netting $75,000 or more get the same paltry amount. In fact, the Gallup numbers Khazan cites reveal that the greater a household's income, the *more* hours per night its members are likely to sleep.[39] Despite tropes of passionate professional workers laboring deep into the night, these figures show that once households have a baseline level of material comfort, they choose to rest instead of wear themselves down with extra work.

Professional, salaried workers tend to draw sufficient wages to meet basic needs from a single job. By contrast, low- and minimum-wage jobs pay so little that workers must string together two or more of these jobs to make ends meet. Khazan chronicles the day of a man in his thirties who works two jobs at John F. Kennedy International Airport. He wakes before dawn to catch a 5 a.m. bus from his apartment in Queens to get to his 7 a.m. shift as an airport wheelchair attendant. He works until 3 p.m., then has a half-hour break before he begins his next job, corralling luggage carts. His second shift ends at 10 p.m., after which he has another long bus ride home, catches a few hours of sleep, and begins again. His two jobs net him about $500 per week. Rather than fulfilled workers whose passion drives them to work into their sleeping hours, it turns out that the workers who sleep the least are those who literally cannot afford a full night's rest, time to nurture relationships, or an hour to pursue other interests. As Khazan puts it, "Though we often praise white-collar 'superwomen' who 'never sleep' and juggle legendary careers with busy families, it's actually people with the least money who get the least amount of sleep."[40]

The myth that Khazan deflates returns us to the questions of visibility and invisibility in the first chapter of this book. Behind every superworker who garners breathless praise for single-handedly, unsleepingly having built something (to use the parlance of Mitt Romney) are the unmentioned service workers who woke up even earlier so that they could pour the white-collar heroes coffee at Starbucks at 6 a.m. or clean out airplane cabins for their 7 a.m. flights. Yes, these crack-of-dawn shifts typically end at midafternoon. Just in time for another shift at another job. Yet it hardly needs mentioning who is celebrated for their hard work and who is not.

Overwork has long been cast as a choice, and a positive one borne out of love at that. But the truth is that for so many, there is no choice. Meeting basic needs such as obtaining food and shelter requires abandoning significant elements of personal care, such as sleep and fostering human relationships. Even though employers have long known that ensuring workers rest and compensating them in a manner that allows them to nurture their whole lives need not have any ill effects on productivity (not to mention being the humane thing to do), the culture of valuing activity purely for its own sake obscures this truth. In fact, quite often, workers clamor for *more* work, so deeply have they internalized their own discipline. The present 24/7 temporality that insists that activity, any activity at all, is preferable to inaction,[41] paired with long-standing prejudices against the poor, people of color, immigrants, and others, provides a schema by which it is possible to valorize certain types of workers who choose to forgo sleep while simultaneously stealing sleep from those who are the poorest and most overworked.

Some must always wake up early or stay up late so that others may work or relax. Numerous ideological lenses exist that allow us to view this reality in favorable ways. Nostalgia allows us to consider the dignified waiter in the Viennese café not as a worker but as an ornament, part of the overall ambiance. DWYL allows us to valorize elite workers, those who choose to overwork, and ignore those who have to overwork. Hopefully, workers will soon be able to look forward to a future in which the romance of overwork is seen for the absurdity it is, in which there's enough sleep to go around.

CONCLUSION

From this hour, I ordain myfself loos'd of limits
and imaginary lines,
Going where I list, my own master total and absolute,
Listening to others, considering well what they say,
Pausing, searching, receiving, contemplating . . .

—Walt Whitman, "Song of the Open Road"
(1856)

Several years ago a friend of mine took a photo of an elderly couple in a park on an autumn day. The woman was in a wheelchair, the man on a bench next to her. They were holding hands and looking at the leaves. They weren't making anything. They weren't buying anything. They weren't doing anything to generate profit or posturing themselves for any kind of monetizeable public self-presentation (their backs were to the camera). They were being wholly unremarkable, but in one way they were exceptional: they were *taking their time*. They were exercising a human right that too many of us forget that we have.

When 100-hour workweeks, a globe roasting in a gaseous oven of carbon and methane emissions, and 85 individuals owning as much as the least wealthy 50 percent of humanity are realities of modern life and not features of some dystopian blockbuster, it's clear that we've reached a number of limits with regard to how we live, work, and consume. The time has come to question some of the most conventional wisdom about the inherent benefits of economic growth and about waged work being the proper conduit for dreaming, loving, realizing our full potential as human beings, and, oh, feeding and sheltering ourselves. Work as a glorious end in itself, it turns out, is a severely limiting worldview, and one that serves workers only rarely. Mantras like "Do what you love" and "Follow your bliss" frequently cloak a ruthless ideology of nonstop production and consumption in the cozy comfort of self-care and pleasure. Yet both of these exhortations, bland as they are, could be quite emancipatory, even radical, if redirected away from work. In fact, as perhaps many readers may have already concluded, they could be directed toward questioning the necessity and centrality of work to our lives.

Why do work? For most, the primary answer is, plainly, for the income, whatever other motivations—service to the community, stewardship of the land, religious obligation, even love—come into play. Our reasons are "multiple and shifting, typically involving a complex blend of coercion and choice, necessity and desire, habit and intention."[1] Nevertheless, few desire to depend on work in order to have a claim to public acknowledgment, to be surveilled and overmanaged, to toil indefinitely in a second-class labor force, or to work through every hour of the clock. A not-insignificant number of workers endure all of the above and still struggle to meet basic needs. And yet these are the very conditions that DWYL in its capitalist form facilitates. Too many have put too much at risk, from human relationships to the natural world, pursuing an out-of-control work ethic.

Working too much and under exploitative conditions has failed to deliver on promises of widespread prosperity (though it has certainly made a few very wealthy) and self-fulfillment. Further, these conditions have despoiled our planet, as Naomi

Klein elucidates in her recent book, *This Changes Everything: Capitalism Versus the Climate*. What is needed, both for individual well-being and the preservation of our natural world, is nothing less than a complete reevaluation of the prevailing attitudes toward and values invested in work. Why, for instance, is it a good thing that mere survival depends on the ability to sell one's labor, day in and day out, on the open market? This seems a vastly preposterous proposition considering the rather large portion of humanity who cannot do this, or who can do it only in limited ways: young children, the elderly, the disabled, the injured, and the sick. In capitalism's purest form, these individuals are utterly without freedom and at the mercy of others selling labor on their behalf.

Why is relentless economic growth to be embraced without question, when it has become obvious that it leaves millions living in appalling conditions and corrodes the planet? Why is work, income aside, more worthy of a person's limited time on Earth than other pursuits? When did time away from work become something not worth fighting for?

The isolated measures to stem overwork, discussed in chapter 4, are an encouraging start to this project of questioning work's preeminence, but they are only a start. Work-limiting schemes such as the Mail on Holiday program and Gothenburg's six-hour workday experiment do little to promote any kind of mass activism beyond small groups of employees. They also do little to dismantle systems of excessive worker surveillance or inequitable tiered labor forces, nor do they challenge the questionable ways in which visibility or invisibility is determined by the work one performs. Finally, these policies, worker-friendly as they are, do not look skeptically at importance of work itself or how it is distributed.

Thinking seriously about what Kathi Weeks terms a "post-work society," that is, not a world in which work is nonexistent, but one in which it is not the central structuring component of our lives, provides a much-needed critical perspective. It is not a given that our basic needs be met via wages, or that work need be the priority around which we allot every other hour of our lives, every other human activity, including sleeping, savoring the company of others, and rearing our children. We've ended up living like this, but we don't have to continue. We can, for instance, demand full employment through equitable distribution of work. This demand reacts directly to realities that the desperate scramble for job creation ignores: that "the system-wide tendency, for almost four decades now, has been to add jobs more slowly than population," yielding societies in which "a proportionally shrinking body of laborers is ever more heavily exploited to ensure a rate of profit that nevertheless continually declines," as Benjamin Kunkel writes. He adds, "Our political demand should be for the opposite arrangement: a larger mass of labor more lightly exploited."[2] This demand puts work back in a subordinate role to humanity. Throughout this book we've seen workers training for jobs that probably won't materialize, inventing make-work for themselves to do, and logging enough hours at one job for three people. Rather than creating more of these jobs without thinking about whether they really move us toward the kind of world we want to pass onto future generations, we should consider how we want people to pass their time in this world.

The freedom made possible by working less and for greater reward shouldn't be relegated to the realm of fantasy. As part of this larger project of equitable work distribution, we can issue other demands for leave periods, sabbaticals, and amply funded public pensions, all of which allow time away from work. The so-called utopian demand is not as easily dismissible as its critics make it seem. Utopian demands for things like drastically reduced working hours provide "tools that can promote distancing from and critical thinking about the present"[3]; exposing conditions once taken for granted as fluid, historically and ideologically determined, and open to skepticism and critique is, as Weeks points out, a useful and important political act.[4] Going further, utopian demands prefigure an alternate world in which the demands themselves would be practical and reasonable.[5] Precisely because that world is outside the present reality, it will appear strange, but it shouldn't necessarily be fearsome. We've already made the world strange by obliterating diurnal cycles of activity and rest and allowing the degradation of our planet for the benefit of a tiny few. Why not make it strange again, but in ways more broadly favorable? Workers had already begun forging this path, and not too long ago. In fact, ever-shorter workdays paired with increasing standards of living once seemed an inevitability. There's no reason why we can't improve upon the great achievements of labor movements past.

Prefiguring a world in which meeting human needs is not entirely dependent on work and the market-driven wage has already begun. Many countries distribute child allowances to families regardless of their work income, to ensure that their youngest citizens are cared for. Finland's famous "baby box," equipped with essentials such as clothing, bath products, and a mattress (the box itself serves as a bassinet) is not mere swag; it also serves as a tangible manifestation of society's promise to welcome and care for its newest members.[6] Even in the comparatively conservative United States, Social Security remains sacrosanct. In fact, letting the free market totally dictate people's ability to support themselves is unpopular in some of the most conservative states in the country. In 2014, voters in Alaska, Arkansas, Nebraska, and South Dakota elected Republicans to the US Senate. In the same election, voters in all four states also overwhelmingly passed ballot initiatives to raise the minimum wage in their states, measures some of their chosen candidates actually opposed. Other municipalities that elected business-friendly Republicans also passed measures guaranteeing paid sick days.[7] What these complex results reveal is that neither major political party currently offers Americans a compelling political agenda regarding the ways in which work meets their needs. The desire for transformational changes in the relationships between work and personal care was sown long ago; it's just obscured by current political structures.

The biggest challenges to advocating for such changes aren't material but cultural. The ingenuity and physical resources exist to create a more equitable, just world. But workers have been disenfranchised and demoralized for so long that bold demands can seem like idle pipe dreams. More fundamental, however, is the seeming inability to imagine a world in which waged labor and material consumption are marginal to people's lives. More work is not needed—it only fuels the short circuit of production and consumption that has yielded economic growth but left a vast amount of the world population living in poverty, deep instability, and squalor. By now it's evident that the more hours workers put in under more exploitative conditions, the more management sees that it can extract from them, and the *less* it is willing to give them in return. So why continue acceding to this dynamic?

If production is due for a reining in, so too is consumption. This does not necessitate an existence of bleak austerity but rather a liberation from the demands of the marketplace. In a rousing essay, Alyssa Battistoni invokes Virginia Woolf, who wrote in "A Room of One's Own" of the banker and the great barrister, trapped indoors, working "to make more money and more money and more money, when it is a fact that five hundred pounds a year will keep a person alive in the sunshine."[8] Consumption, though it offers fleeting hits of pleasure, is nothing but a snare continuously dragging us back to the grindstone. Consumption is the opposite of freedom—the more we consume, the more time we have to spend in desperate pursuit of wealth, which for most of us means more of our lives spent at work.

The word *freedom*, particularly over the last decade and a half, has become so overused as to be nearly meaningless. Ironically, it presents often in the severely limited form of consumerism—the freedom to choose iced tea or lemonade, iPhone or Blackberry—all for which we must spend time working. But outside of the marketplace, freedom takes on awesome, almost limitless proportions: freedom to daydream, to give love and care to others, to amble through nature and neighborhoods, to listen and debate.

If the idea of finding value in states of being other than work still sounds alarming, Battistoni points out that such schemes already exist even within mainstream environmental economics. Payment-for-ecosystems (PES) programs price ecological functions, such as pollination, that, like housework, capitalism had taken to be free. While the actual implementation of PES programs leaves much to be desired—Battistoni notes that value collected from ecosystems often ends up in the traditional hands of local power structures—at their core, they represent "the first step in a broader project in changing the way we think about the relationship between human society and the natural world."[9] Despite their envelopment into a neoliberal schema, PES programs are remarkable in that they "recognize the value of *not* working, of *not* producing, as in programs that pay people not to cut down trees—compensating them for lost income in the name of global sustainability." In other words, we are *already* paying some people *not* to work because it's in our own self-interest. Why not extend that practice?

It's not like there's a lot of work that needs doing, yet we still insist on making even more of it. In *Young Money*, Kevin Roose describes the farcical but all-too-real scenario in which rookie financial analysts fresh out of expensive colleges and universities stay in the office all hours of the night, grinding out "pitch books" (packets in which banks propose potential deals to clients), many of which never get read. In other words, some of their (highly compensated and demanding) work is, from the moment of its completion, garbage.[10] Yet it is the fast-food worker who is scorned for demanding fifteen dollars per hour, even though the fruit of his or her labor—a hot meal—can often be consumed in a more meaningful way. Co-incidentally, one of the elite young analysts Roose chronicled calculated his income—including a reasonable estimate of his yearly bonus—broken down by hour; it came to around sixteen dollars an hour after taxes.[11]

Such inefficiencies are everywhere: across the globe, the agriculture industry burns fuel planting, growing, and harvesting crops no one will eat; the construction industry builds homes no one will live in. Every Dumpster diver knows that behind every big-box store are piles of discarded, never-opened sundries like shampoo and Christmas lights. Well-made rotary telephones lasted for decades; now, manufacturers ensure that you will have to replace your smartphone in five years, if not sooner. Someone was paid (however appallingly little) and spent hours away from their loved ones and other interests in order to make these things. Despite these excesses, unemployment remains a worldwide problem. In parts of southern Europe, around 50 percent of young people are without jobs. Patrick Spät points out in his critique of contemporary work culture that there is hardly a campaigning politician who doesn't promise more jobs,[12] but is more work really the solution? Why have the unemployed do eight hours of waste-generating make-work per day just to feed themselves?

Viewed in this light, the value of *not* producing comes into clearer focus. Why not get to work distributing the resources we have instead of producing more crap no one needs or even wants, just so a fortunate few can skim profits off of the production process? Why not invest in the caring work—parenting and childcare, elder care, teaching, and nursing—that must be done no matter what? And while we're at it, why not broadly distribute this work, too, so that it doesn't become an overwhelming burden to anyone as it is today for so many?

The resources exist to provide most of humanity with humane living conditions. But capitalism isn't dedicated to meeting needs efficiently. Rather, as we've seen time and again, the opposite is true, despite the highly regimented mass ornament aesthetics. Neil deGrasse Tyson mentions in his television series, *Cosmos: A Spacetime Odyssey*, that solar radiation bathes our planet with free energy, more than we will ever need. Yet instead of working as hard as possible to capture and store this energy, we dawdle while continuing to pay oil, coal, and natural gas companies so we can burn fossil fuels at great cost—a cost not only financial, but human, borne out by the tragedies of colonialization, slavery, and war unleashed by our relentless thirst for energy. Other examples of such absurdity abound. Rich municipalities pay to transport food waste to landfills while millions languish in malnutrition and hunger. Verdant golf courses dot the arid regions of the United States while citizens in Detroit have their water shut off.

If a work ethic has brought about these inequities, then

it's time to search for a new one. Fortunately, auspicious and optimistic models already exist. Both Virginia Woolf and Walt Whitman offer alternative ethics of freedom in its broadest sense—to live and think openly. Battistoni notes that Woolf's own "five hundred pounds a year" allowed her to think and write as she pleased. Whitman, in his "Song of the Open Road," espouses the endless fascination of sensing the world, interacting with its people, "pausing, searching, receiving, contemplating." Whereas René Descartes declared matter-of-factly, "I am a thinking thing," Whitman is thrilled by his consciousness, as Hunnicutt beautifully describes: "Consciousness of consciousness, awareness of the freedom of awareness astounds and delights the soul, offering it infinite employment. . . ."[13] Against the propositions of both writers, the idea of DWYL as pertaining to waged labor utterly diminishes and reveals itself to be severely constricted. The only prerequisites for enjoying the freedoms that Woolf and Whitman describe are resources for basic personal care and time. These are things we can give one another, if we choose to.

NOTES

INTRODUCTION

1 Pamela H. Smith, *The Body of the Artisan: Art and Experience in the Scientific Revolution* (Chicago: University of Chicago Press, 2004), 214.

2 Michelangelo, "To Giovanni da Pistoia," trans. Joel Agee, *The New York Review of Books*, June 19, 2014. www.nybooks.com/articles/archives/2014/jun/19/giovanni-da-pistoia/

3 Robert Pinksy, "Labor Pains," *Slate*, January 26, 2010. www.slate.com/articles/arts/poem/2010/01/labor_pains.html

4 Michael Baxandall, *Painting and Experience in Fifteenth-Century Italy*, 2nd ed. (Oxford: Oxford University Press, 1988), 1.

5 Thomas Jefferson, *Notes on the State of Virginia*, 290 (TKPublisher Info).

6 John Mackey and Marc Gafni, "A Conversation with John Mackey & Marc Gafni—Topic 4." July 7, 2014, www.youtube.com/watch?v=Hgz-rvgBlS30#

7 Miya Tokumitsu, "In the Name of Love," *Jacobin* 13 (2014).

8 Max Weber, *The Protestant Ethic and the Spirit of Capitalism*, ed. Richard Swedberg (W.W. Norton & Co. Inc., 2009), 24.

9 Weber (2009), 26.

10 Benjamin Kline Hunnicutt, *Free Time: The Forgotten American Dream* (Philadelphia: Temple University Press, 1996), 34.

11 Nikil Saval, *Cubed: A Secret History of the Office* (New York: Doubleday, 2014), 34.

12 Tom Wolfe, "The 'Me' Decade and the Third Great Awakening," *New York* magazine, August 23, 1976. nymag.com/news/features/45938/

13 Wolfe (1976).

14 Wolfe, (1976).

15 Aaron Braun, "Dispatches from the Labor Market," *Full Stop*, July 16, 2014. www.full-stop.net/2014/07/16/features/essays/aaron-braun/dispatches-from-the-labor-market/

16 Peter Jacobs, "There Are Now 50 Colleges That Charge More Than $60,000 Per Year," *Business Insider*, July 10, 2014. www.businessinsider.com/50-colleges-charge-60000-dollars-2014-7

17 David Leonhardt, "Is College Worth It? Clearly, the Data Say," *The New York Times*, The Upshot, May 27, 2014. www.nytimes.com/2014/05/27/upshot/is-college-worth-it-clearly-new-data-say.html?abt=0002&abg=0

18 Leonhardt (2014).

19 Robert Reich, "Why College Is Necessary but Gets You Nowhere," *Guernica*, November 25, 2014. www.guernicamag.com/daily/robert-reich-why-college-is-necessary-but-gets-you-nowhere/

20 Reich (2014).

21 Reich (2014).

22 Laya Anasu and Michael D. Ledecky, "Freshmen Survey Part II: An Uncommon App," *Harvard Crimson*, September 4, 2013. www.thecrimson.com/article/2013/9/4/freshman-survey-admissions-aid/

23 Chris Maisano, "The Soul of Student Debt," *Jacobin* 9 (2012). www.jacobinmag.com/2012/12/the-soul-of-student-debt/

24 Maisano (2012).

25 Maisano (2012).

26 Kevin Roose, *Young Money: Inside the Hidden World of Wall Street's Post-Crash Recruits* (New York: Grand Central Publishing, 2014), ix.

27 Lynn Stuart Parramore, "Cut-Throat Capitalism: Welcome to the

Gig Economy," *Alternet*, May 27, 2014. www.alternet.org/economy/
cut-throat-capitalism-welcome-gig-economy

28 Ned Resnikoff, "Yoga Teachers: Overstretched and Underpaid,"
MSNBC, July 7, 2014. www.msnbc.com/msnbc/yoga-teachers-over-
stretched-and-underpaid

CHAPTER 1

1 Jonathan Crary, *24/7: Late Capitalism and the Ends of Sleep* (New York:
Verso, 2013), 21–22, 33.

2 Crary (2013), 30.

3 Crary (2013), 21–22; Hannah Arendt, *The Human Condition*, 2nd ed.
(Chicago, University of Chicago Press, 1958), 133–134.

4 George Packer, "Where Have All the Workers Gone?" *The New Yorker*,
February 24, 2014. www.newyorker.com/online/blogs/
comment/2014/02/where-have-all-the-workers-gone.html

5 Karen Beckman, *Vanishing Women: Magic, Film, and Feminism*
(Durham, NC: Duke University Press, 2003), 156.

6 Silvia Federici, "Putting Feminism Back on Its Feet" (1984). Reprinted
in Silvia Federici, *Revolution at Point Zero* (Oakland, CA: PM Press,
2012), 57.

7 Dionne Searcey, "Women Quit Jobs in Peak Years, Setback for Them
and Economy," *The New York Times*, June 24, 2014.

8 Searcey (2014).

9 Rose Lichter-Marck, "Vivian Maier and the Problem of Difficult
Women," *The New Yorker*, May 9, 2014.

10 Arendt (1958), 71.

11 Crary (2013), 129-30.

12 Zadie Smith, "Generation Why?" *The New York Review of Books*,
November 25, 2010. www.nybooks.com/articles/archives/2010/
nov/25/generation-why/?page=1

CHAPTER 2

1 Noam Chomsky, "The Death of American Universities." Address to the Adjunct Faculty Association of the United Steelworkers, Pittsburgh, PA, February 2014. www.jacobinmag.com/2014/03/the-death-of-american-universities/

2 Danielle Muoio, "That Comcast Customer Service Rep Wasn't Going Rogue," *Businessweek*, July 18, 2014.

3 John Herrman, "Sympathy for the Comcast Rep from Hell," *The Awl*, July 15, 2014.

4 Steve Lohr, "Unblinking Eyes Track Employees," *The New York Times*, June 21, 2014.

5 Ben Warber as told to Joshua Brustein, "The Case for Wearing Productivity Sensors on the Job," *Bloomberg Business*, December 19, 2013. www.bloomberg.com/bw/articles/2013-12-19/sociometric-solutions-ben-warber-on-workers-wearing-sensors

6 Warber to Brustein (2013).

7 Lohr (2014).

8 Carl Cederström and Paul Fleming, *Dead Man Working* (Winchester, UK: Zero Books, 2012), 7.

9 Lohr (2014).

10 Lohr (2014).

11 David Welna, "NSA Implementing Fix to Prevent Snowden-Like Security Breach," National Public Radio report, July 11, 2014.

12 Frédéric Lordon, *Willing Slaves of Capital: Spinoza & Marx on Desire*, trans. Gabriel Ash (New York: Verso, 2014), 51–52.

13 Barbara and John Ehrenreich, "The Professional-Managerial Class," *Radical America* 11, no. 2 (1977), 13.

14 Ehrenreich (1977), 18–19.

15 Ehrenreich (1977), 15, 22.

16 Ehrenreich (1977), 21–22.

17 Ehrenreich (1977), 20–22.

18 Saval (2014), 47.

19 Barbara and John Ehrenreich, *Death of a Yuppie Dream: The Rise and Fall of the Professional-Managerial Class* (New York: Rosa Luxemburg Stiftung, 2013), 9.

20 Valerie Strauss, "Mom: My Kindergartner Was 'Work-Sheeted to Death,'" *Washington Post*, July 19, 2014. www.washingtonpost.com/blogs/answer-sheet/wp/2014/07/19/mom-my-kindergartner-was-work-sheeted-to-death/

21 Edward Miller and Joan Almon, "Crisis in the Kindergarten: Why Children Need to Play in School" (College Park, MD: Alliance for Childhood, 2009), 39.

22 Miller and Almon (2009), 39–41.

23 Miller and Almon (2009), 41; National Association of School Psychologists, "Position Statement: Early Childhood Assessment," 2009. www.nasponline.org/about_nasp/positionpapers/Early ChildhoodAssessment.pdf

24 Miller and Almon (2009), 40–41.

25 The National Commission on Excellence in Education, *A Nation at Risk: The Imperative for Educational Reform. A Report to the Nation and to the Secretary of Education United States Department of Education.* April 1983, p. 9. See also Megan Erickson, "A Nation of Little Lebowski Urban Achievers," *Jacobin* 5 (2011). www.jacobinmag.com/2011/12/a-nation-of-little-lebowski-urban-achievers/

26 Rachel Aviv, "Wrong Answer," *The New Yorker*, July 21, 2014. www.newyorker.com/magazine/2014/07/21/wrong-answer

27 Sarah Jaffe, "Massachusetts Teachers Aim to Knock Down 'Data Walls,'" *In These Times*, February 12, 2014. inthesetimes.com/working/entry/16276/massachusetts_teachers_knock_down_data_walls

28 Diane Ravitch, "No Student Left Untested," *The New York Review of Books*, February 21, 2012.

29 Shawn Gude, "The Industrial Classroom," *Class Action: An Activist Teacher's Handbook* (Bronx, NY: Jacobin Foundation, 2014), 21–31.

30 Aviv (2014).

31 Gary Stern, "Some School Districts Nix 'Field Tests,'" *The Journal News*, June 3, 2014. www.lohud.com/story/news/2014/06/02/school-districts-nix-field-tests/9895867/

32 PBS and *Frontline*, *The Testing Industry's Big Four*. www.pbs.org/wgbh/pages/frontline/shows/schools/testing/companies.html

33 LynNell Hancock, "Why Are Finland's Schools Successful?" *Smithsonian Magazine*, September 2011. www.smithsonianmag.com/innovation/why-are-finlands-schools-successful-49859555/?c=y%3Fno-ist

34 Hancock (2011).

35 Hancock (2011).

36 Saval (2014), 29–32.

37 Cederström and Fleming (2012), 4.

38 Benjamin Ginsburg, *The Fall of the Faculty: The Rise of the All-Administrative University and Why it Matters* (Oxford: Oxford University Press, 2011), 43.

39 Ginsburg (2011), 42.

40 Ginsburg (2011), 14.

41 Ginsburg (2011), 43.

42 Ginsburg (2011), 13–15, 36–37.

43 Ginsburg (2011), 35.

44 Gallup, "State of the American Workplace," 12.

45 Jenny Diski, "Post-Its, Push Pins, Pencils," *London Review of Books*, 36, no. 15 (July 31, 2014), 3–7.

46 Diski (2014), 3–7.

47 Lordon, xi–xii.

48 Rachel L. Swarns, "Freelancers in the 'Gig Economy' Find a Mix of

Freedom and Uncertainty," *The New York Times*, February 9, 2014.

49 Gerald Friedman, interviewed by Lynn Stuart Parramore, "Cut-Throat Capitalism: Welcome to the Gig Economy," *Alternet*, May 27, 2014.

CHAPTER 3

1 Emily, Vassar College, "7 Internship Success Tips from a 4-Time Fashion Intern," *College Fashion*, January 8, 2012. www.collegefashion .net/college-life/7-internship-success-tips-from-a-4-time-fashion-in-tern/

2 Madeleine Schwartz, "Opportunity Costs: The True Price of Internships," *Dissent* (Winter 2013). www.dissentmagazine.org/article/ opportunity-costs-the-true-price-of-internships

3 Ross Perlin, *Intern Nation: How to Earn Nothing and Learn Little in the Brave New Economy* (New York: Verso, 2012), xiv, 28.

4 Kathleen Kuehn, "Why Do So Many Journalists Write for Free?" *The Canadian Journalism Project*, February 3, 2014.

5 Marc Bousquet, "We Work," *The Minnesota Review* 71–72 (Winter/ Spring 2009), 149–50.

6 Kathleen Kuehn and Thomas F. Corrigan, "Hope Labor: The Role of Employment Prospects in Online Social Production," *The Political Economy of Communication* 1:1 (2013), 9–25.

7 Kuehn and Corrigan (2013), 14–15.

8 Perlin (2012), 75.

9 Alex Williams, "For Interns, All Work and No Payoff," *The New York Times*, February 14, 2014. www.nytimes.com/2014/02/16/fashion/ millennials-internships.html

10 Yuki Noguchi, "An Intern at 40-Something, and 'Paid in Hugs,'" National Public Radio report, April 1, 2014. www.npr.org/2014/04/01/293882686/ an-intern-at-40-something-and-paid-in-hugs

11 Perlin (2012), 66.

12 Perlin (2012), 78–82.

13 Intern Bridge, Inc., "The Debate over Unpaid College Internships," 6. www.ceri.msu.edu/wp-content/uploads/2010/01/Intern-Bridge-Unpaid-College-Internship-Report-FINAL.pdf; Perlin (2012), 26.

14 Schwartz (2013).

15 Faith Guvenen et al., "What Do Data on Millions of US Workers Reveal About Life Cycle Earnings Risk?" *Federal Reserve Bank of New York Staff Reports*, no. 710 (February 2015), 13; Akane Otani, "Your Lifetime Earnings Are Decided in the First 10 Years of Your Career," *Bloomberg Business*, February 10, 2015. www.bloomberg.com/news/articles/2015-02-09/your-lifetime-earnings-are-decided-in-the-first-10-years-of-your-career

16 Guvenen et al. (2015), 13.

17 Otani (2015).

18 "The High Cost of Adjunct Living: Boston" (Adjunct Action white paper, SEIU). campaign-media.seiumedia.net.s3.amazonaws.com/wp-content/uploads/2013/11/17694-White-paper-FINAL.pdf

19 House Committee on Education and the Workforce, Democratic Staff, "The Just-in-Time Professor: A Staff Report Summarizing the eForum Responses on the Working Conditions of Contingent Faculty in Higher Education," January 2014, 25.

20 House Committee on Education and the Workforce (2014), 25.

21 Richard Harris, "Too Few University Jobs for America's Young Scientists," National Public Radio report, September 16, 2014. www.npr.org/blogs/health/2014/09/16/343539024/too-few-university-jobs-for-americas-young-scientists?sc=ipad&f=1001

22 Rob Bryan, "Disposable Goods: On Overcoming the Temp Industry," *Jacobin*, October 2, 2013. www.jacobinmag.com/2013/10/disposable-goods/

23 Bryan (2013).

24 Erin Hatton, *The Temp Economy: From Kelly Girls to Permatemps in Postwar America* (Philadelphia: Temple University Press, 2011), 148.

25 Hatton (2011), 49–54.

26 Hatton (2011), 19.

27 Hatton (2011), 20–21.

28 Hatton (2011), 11.

29 Sarah Jaffe, "Forever Temp?" *In These Times*, January 6, 2014. inthese times.com/article/15972/permatemps_in_manufacturing

30 Jaffe (2014).

31 Michael Grabell and Lena Groeger, "Temp Worker Regulations Around the World." *ProPublica*, February 24, 2014. projects .propublica.org/graphics/temps-around-the-world

32 Stephen Greenhouse, "Judge Rules That Movie Studio Should Have Been Paying Interns," *The New York Times*, June 11, 2013. www .nytimes.com/2013/06/12/business/judge-rules-for-interns-who-sued-fox-searchlight.html

33 ProPublica database of intern lawsuits: projects.propublica.org/ graphics/intern-suits

34 Vanessa Thorpe, "London Fashion Week Demonstration Will High-light Plight of Industry's Unpaid Interns," *The Observer*, February 9, 2013.

35 Michael Grabell, "California Legislature Passes Bill to Protect Temp Workers." *ProPublica*, August 29, 2014.

36 Sheet Metal Workers International Association Web site, "Media and Policy Makers: About Us." www.smwia.org/Media-and-Policy-Makers.aspx

37 Perlin (2012), 109.

38 Marc Bousquet, "Offensive Letter Justifies Oppressive System That Hurts Both Faculty and Students," *The Chronicle of Higher*

Education, August 29, 2014. chronicle.com/article/Offensive-Letter-Justifies/148551/

CHAPTER 4

1 Crary (2013), 25

2 Roose (2014), 132.

3 Sarah Leonard, "She Can't Sleep No More," *Jacobin* 9 (2012). www.jacobinmag.com/2012/12/she-cant-sleep-no-more/

4 Kathleen Geier, "Our Dangerous Culture of Overwork," *The Baffler*, June 13, 2014.

5 Geier (2014).

6 Sara Robinson, "Why We Have to Go Back to a 40-Hour Workweek to Keep Our Sanity," *Alternet*, March 13, 2012. www.alternet.org/story/154518/why_we_have_to_go_back_to_a_40-hour_work_week_to_keep_our_sanity

7 Robinson (2012); Evan Robinson, "Why Crunch Mode Doesn't Work: Six Lessons" (white paper), International Game Developers Association, 2005.

8 Robinson (2012).

9 Robinson (2012).

10 Robinson (2012).

11 Tony Schwartz and Christine Porath, "Why You Hate Work," *The New York Times*, May 30, 2014. www.nytimes.com/2014/06/01/opinion/sunday/why-you-hate-work.html

12 Schwartz and Porath (2014).

13 Cederström and Fleming (2012), 16–17.

14 Cederström and Fleming (2012), 36.

15 Gilles Deleuze, "Postscript on the Societies of Control," *October*, 59 (1992), 4.

16 Deleuze (1992), 5.

17 Kathi Weeks, *The Problem with Work: Feminism, Marxism, Antiwork Politics, and Postwork Imaginaries* (Durham, NC: Duke University Press, 2011), 53.

18 Crary (2013), 72.

19 Benjamin Kline Hunnicutt, *Free Time: The Forgotten American Dream* (Philadelphia: Temple University Press, 2013), vii.

20 Hunnicutt, 96–102.

21 John Maynard Keynes, "Economic Possibilities for Our Grandchildren" (1930) in John Maynard Keynes, *Essays in Persuasion* (New York: W. W. Norton & Co., 1963), 361.

22 Keynes (1963), 363.

23 Hunnicutt (2013), 52.

24 Hunnicutt (2013), 149.

25 Hunnicutt (2013), 160.

26 Hunnicutt (2013), 154.

27 Ronald Edsforth, "Why Automation Didn't Shorten the Work Week: The Politics of Work Time in the Auto Industry." In *Autowork*, ed. Robert Asher and Ronald Edsforth (Albany, NY: State University of New York Press, 1995), 168.

28 Karl Marx, *Grundrisse*. www.marxists.org/archive/marx/works/1857/grundrisse/ch10.htm

29 Crary (2013), 64–65.

30 Siegfried Kracauer, "The Mass Ornament" (1927) in Siegfried Kracauer, *The Mass Ornament: Weimar Essays*, ed. and trans. Thomas Y. Levin (Cambridge, MA: Harvard University Press, 1995), 78.

31 Kracauer (1995), 78.

32 Weeks (2011), 45.

33 Weeks (2011), 45.

34 "When the French Clock Off at 6pm, They Really Mean It," *The Guardian*, Shortcuts blog, April 4, 2014. www.theguardian.com/

money/shortcuts/2014/apr/09/french-6pm-labour-agreement-work-emails-out-of-office

35 Rebecca J. Rosen, "Daimler Employees Can Set Email to Auto-Delete During Vacation." *The Atlantic*, August 14, 2014. www.theatlantic .com/business/archive/2014/08/daimlers-german-employees-can-set-emails-to-auto-delete-during-vacation/376068/

36 Denis Campbell, "UK Needs Four-Day Week to Combat Stress, Says Top Doctor," *The Guardian*, July 1, 2014. www.theguardian.com/ society/2014/jul/01/uk-four-day-week-combat-stress-top-doctor

37 Kristyn Martin, "Inside a Company That Works a 4-Day Work Week," Al Jazeera America, June 30, 2014. america.aljazeera.com/watch/ shows/real-money-with-alivelshi/articles/2014/6/30/inside-the-life-ofacompanythatworksa4workweek.html

38 Martin (2014).

39 Olga Khazan, "When You Can't Afford to Sleep." *The Atlantic*, September 15, 2014. www.theatlantic.com/health/archive/2014/09/when-you-cant-afford-sleep/380128/

40 Khazan (2014).

41 Crary (2013), 45.

CONCLUSION

1 Weeks (2011), 37–38.

2 Benjamin Kunkel, *Utopia or Bust: A Guide to the Present Crisis* (New York: Verso, 2014), 81.

3 Weeks (2011), 225.

4 Weeks (2011), 176.

5 Weeks (2011), 176.

6 Helena Lee, "Why Finnish Babies Sleep in Cardboard Boxes," *BBC News Magazine* June 4, 2013. www.bbc.com/news/magazine-22751415

7 Brigid Schulte, "Even in Some Red States, Voters Overwhelmingly

Approve Paid Sick Days, Minimum Wage Hikes," *The Washington Post*, November 5, 2014. www.washingtonpost.com/blogs/she-the-people/ wp/2014/11/05/even-in-some-red-states-voters-overwhelmingly-approve-paid-sick-days-minimum-wage-hikes/

8 Alyssa Battistoni, "Alive in the Sunshine," *Jacobin* 13 (Winter 2013). www. jacobinmag.com/2014/01/alive-in-the-sunshine/. Virginia Woolf, *A Room of One's Own* (Adelaide: The University of Adelaide Library) E-book, 71–72. ebooks.adelaide.edu.au/w/woolf/virginia/w91r/

9 Battistoni (2013).

10 Roose (2014), 113–114.

11 Roose (2014), 114.

12 Patrick Spät, "Ich arbeite, so bin ich," *Die Zeit*, July 21, 2014. www .zeit.de/karriere/beruf/2014-07/gastbeitrag-arbeit-sinn

13 Hunnicutt (2013), 53.

Index